When It Happens

When It Happens

An Anthology of Creative Nonfiction

Collected and edited by Rebecca Brenner,
Dani Buchner, Shoshana Green and Ken Levine

LIFE RATTLE PRESS TORONTO, CANADA

When It Happens
An Anthology of Creative Nonfiction

Collected and edited by: Rebecca Brenner, Dani Buchner,
Shoshana Green and Ken Levine

Published by Life Rattle Press, Toronto, Canada
First Canadian Edition

Copyright © 2016 by contributing authors:
Rebecca Brenner
Keith Brown
Dani Buchner
Sandra Campoverde
Heba Elsherief
Candice Frederick
Michael Graham
Shoshana Green
Ken Levine
Alesia Malec
Laura Raymond
Aya Nishiyama
Loredana Polidoro
Deena Kara Shaffer
Martha Sinclair
Stefanie Turner

ISBN 978-1-987936-26-1

Life Rattle New Writers series

Cover Illustration by: Lena Spoke

Contents

Forward

For twelve Monday evenings beginning in January, the 2015 Expressive Writing Collective composed, discussed, and edited their creative nonfiction under the leadership of Guy Allen.

We wrote stories each week—sad stories, being bad stories, wild, thrilling, woo-hoo stories, stories of love, strife, friendship, childhood gone wrong, childhood heroics, family life, work life, everyday life, and no life.

Four of us—Rebecca, Dani, Shoshan and Ken—decided to collect stories to build this anthology. These stories reveal "When It Happens."

The *When It Happens* Editing Team
Toronto, Canada
April 2016

Compass

Aya Nishiyama

S hoot. I can't find it.

I rummage through my backpack. I peek into my desk. I march to the back of the classroom and check my cubby. I can't find my purple compass.

Warm spring sunshine beams through the windows of Kasuga Elementary School. The stained curtains catch the wind, inflate, and lie still. I gaze at the clock above the blackboard at the front of the classroom. Seven minutes remain before math class begins.

Mrs. Nihei, our 4th grade homeroom teacher, nags and yells at people who forget things. I've seen her victims. She asks them to stand up. Everybody stares. Embarrassment reddens the victim's face and their eyes dart about. Mrs. Nihei reports to the victim's parents. I can't let that happen to me.

The clock ticks. Class begins in five minutes. My palms sweat. My heart pumps. I scan the brown wooden floor that we swept after lunch. I spot some white chalk powder, eraser crumbs, and dust.

I glance over the neighbouring desks and observe the lines of purple compasses. We each use the same purple and black compass, distributed by the school. A sharp steel needle sticks out at the end. A white plastic container protects the compass from shocks. I observe many dents in the white plastic containers.

My eyes stop at Seki-kun's desk, two seats in front of mine. Seki-kun forgets something every day. Today, his compass sits on his desk.

The clock ticks. Sweat streams down my face. I pace up to Seki-kun's desk. I confirm that no one watches me. I reach out my arm. I feel the cool plastic container in my palm. The bell rings. I slip back to my desk.

"Please take out your compass," Mrs. Nihei announces. "I want it at the top-right corner of your desk."

Seki-kun's black, curly hair swings side to side, "What!? Where is it?"

Mrs. Nihei's beautiful smile becomes an evil grimace, "Did you forget your compass again?"

"No, Miss, I had it on my desk! I brought it at last! I—"

"Don't make excuses, Seki-kun."

"But, Miss, I did bring it! It was on my desk a few minutes ago, and—"

"Enough, enough. I don't want to hear it anymore. Now stand up!"

I ease Seki-kun's compass to the top-right corner of my desk. I make sure that Seki-kun's name faces down. A cool breeze brushes my neck. My heart slows. I direct my eyes from the compass, to Seki-kun, to Mrs. Nihei, then to some dust floating in the air. Sunshine filters through the window. The clock ticks.

Should I Cry?

Rebecca Brenner

Maia giggles, "I should've put some stage makeup on." I reassure her that no one will see the video I record of us on my computer.

We conduct our interview by Skype and begin at 10:00 p.m. on March 6, 2015. Maia didn't want to take the Go train downtown in this snowy weather. And Maia keeps busy with her triple career as social worker, storyteller, and expressive arts therapy student. Last year, we met every Thursday in Kensington Market for vegan food at Hibiscus Cafe and gossip. Maia would describe her latest fling, and I would try not to sound too self-satisfied about my stable relationship. Maia's guys always turned out to be spoiled or creepy or misogynist or mean.

"I want it to be a story I don't already know. So I can be excited to hear it for the first time," I say.

"I think you know all my stories," Maia begins. She grins, and I think back to the time we sat in Moonbean Cafe just before closing and Maia told me about the guy she met on the bus who ended up being gay and how she almost slept with him and then she found out he had a boyfriend and was just trying 'a girl', and we both laughed so hard that we knocked over my matcha latte and it cascaded all over the worn wooden floor, and the people around us swivelled to watch. Maia and I couldn't stop giggling.

"No, not the guy stories," I fix my teeth together in a smile. "Something else?"

Maia fiddles with the tips of her thigh-length black hair, holding one lock up to her cheek. She scrunches her nose to the side.

I wave my arms around, "Well, I guess I wanted to hear the whole story of what, of what happened in your childhood with all the moving and, and all that. Is . . ." I run my tongue over my top lip and bite down. I breathe in, "Is there a place where you want to begin?"

"You choose any place and I'll begin there," Maia says.

Maia wears bright colours and projects her words in a loud, musical voice. She articulates with her hands and tosses her hair from side to side as punctuation. When we're together, other people join our conversations. Maia knows how to make people feel comfortable. And yet I don't know how to ask Maia about her childhood.

I remember when I first saw Maia. We both sat in a common room at our expressive arts therapy school in England. I chatted with two other girls. Maia perched on a couch, alone, her hair curved around her shoulders, and her crimson red cat's-eye glasses brought out the bright blackness of her eyes.

"I was wondering," I say. "People's childhoods don't necessarily start out atypical. There's usually a time when things go off on a different path and suddenly you're not the 'normal' kid with the 'normal' childhood anymore. So," I grimace, "maybe we could start there?"

Maia arches backwards and tilts her head, "Well, actually, that's something I think about a lot because I'm not sure if it was an actual event or if I was atypical before the event."

I wonder whether I will manage to have Maia open up about her childhood at last.

Maia smiles, lips pursed, and continues, "I was a severely shy child. Oh so shy. When my mother and I would go out, I would hide behind her skirt. And I was really antisocial. I wouldn't play with other children."

Maia glances up, eyelids low. I nod her on.

"I was born in Libya, and in Libya you don't have to go to kindergarten if your mom stays at home. My mom stayed home. So it was a rare occasion when I played with other children and that was fine by me. So I was always a bit different from other children."

The video cuts out on my end. I fiddle with Skype. I shut Skype down and return online.

Before I can say sorry for the cut, Maia speaks, "I always had my intense personality. Well, psychologists say you're born with your personality. I was quite a creative little kid. But things changed. I guess the landmark of when things really changed would have been when the 1986 bombing of Libya happened." Maia shrugs. Her shrug seems apologetic, and I try to understand why Maia would ask my forgiveness for a bombing where she was the victim.

"I was six years old and, before that, we were moving around a lot. I moved to Jordan when I was six months old and we lived there until I was a year and a half. My father and my uncle had a business, and my uncle ended up gambling away their whole business, and we had to move to Croatia—it was Yugoslavia then—and later we moved back to Libya."

We both giggle.

Last July we hobbled along Augusta Avenue, and we guffawed so hard about the way our critical theory teacher in England liked eating 'peaches with tea' that we decided to enter the Hot Box Cafe so we would have an excuse for laughing.

Maia smiles, "So we were back in Libya when I was six years old in 1986."

She stutters, "The bombing happened. Well, it was missiles. It was 2:00 in the morning. My parents kind of were prepared because, for two weeks before that, there was lots of talk and threats of bombing. So we were sleeping in my parents' room all together. It was 2:00 a.m. and the windows burst open and I woke up and, and having a different personality from most children, I wasn't really that bothered because my father had told me we would be bombed."

Maia mimics her father, "We're probably gonna be bombed, and you might die," and she cracks up and squeaks when she laughs.

"My father had grown up in political violence so he was very honest. And so when it happened, I wasn't crying or anything." She flicks her hand to the side, fingertips last, "Does a six year old really know what death is?"

I think about this. When I was six, my cat Damocles had FIDS, the feline form of AIDS, but I thought it was just a bad cold, and I thought it was funny when Damocles sneezed big yellow blobs of mucus on boys when they came to my house and played with him. When I was six, I'd already forgotten about my maternal grandfather who died three years earlier.

"I remember my mom taking us to the window. It was a big balcony window such as this," Maia points behind her and reaches to draw the curtain aside. I glimpse dark burgundy and black shadows that blend together.

"She took me to the window, and my brother, and she pointed to the explosions, which were still taking place, and she said, 'No, we're not being bombed. It's just fireworks.'"

I exclaim, "She said what?!"

"Yeah, she said that to my brother so he'd calm down. Now, as an adult looking back on it, I really have to give it to my mother," Maia beams.

"And so then, we went downstairs to the basement and—" Maia catches my gaze. "When I tell the story, it's always in the same way. I always remember those details in the same way. But, you know, with trauma, it tends to repeat. It repeats itself in the same way all the time, so that could also be it. But the memories are apparently correct because my parents are actually quite amazed at how accurately I remember it. But the facts are always in the same order when I tell it and the same things always stick out."

I want Maia to tell the story, not justify it, and I scrunch up my forehead and nod in an attempt to mask my frustration.

"There are other things I could talk about," Maia stares into her camera lens, "but I don't."

"Of course," I say. I open my eyes wide to show I believe her.

"So, we went down to the basement and everybody, everybody was crying and there were just so many people, lined up on the floor. People were lined up on the floor."

"Oh, oh," I interrupt. "How did more people get into your house?"

"Oh, sorry. We lived in an apartment building on the fifth floor."

I rearrange my mental image.

Maia rocks back and forth on her sit-bones and recrosses her legs. I wonder if she is getting tired or bored.

I encourage her, "Oh?"

Maia releases her breath and feels her forehead, "So we went downstairs and everybody was crying and people were sitting on mattresses on the floor and some on the bare floor and everybody's crying and I'm still not crying and my brother's still shaking with tears. Then, I remember looking in front of me and, in the chaos of the whole situation, all that I could see was a little girl who had legs curved like this."

Maia waves her hands in front of her and ripples them down in curves. She twists her face to the side, "And I remember thinking, 'This little girl has snakes for legs.' And I turned around to my mother and I said, 'Oo—' I said in Croatian, 'Why are her legs like that?' And my mom brushed me off really fast, saying, 'Because she was born that way.' And then my mom went back to dealing with the situation."

Maia stares into the screen, her eyes unfocused, "I sat there and stared at the snake-leg girl. I didn't look away. And I remember thinking later how that little girl helped me because I would have, probably, been more focused on the bombings if she hadn't been there. And, to this day, when I think back on that event, I think back to that little girl with snakes for legs!"

Maia shakes her upper body, then sinks back into the pillows of her couch. She closes her eyes. I'm not sure if it's static from Skype, but I think a teardrop skims Maia's cheek.

Maia jerks upright, smile back in place, "I wonder now if the reason I work with people with disabilities, why I'm passionate about that topic, is because of that little girl! I don't know," Maia chuckles at her own ingenuous connection. "But, anyway, then I remembered that people were still crying and I turned to my brother and I asked him, I said, 'Everybody's crying. Should I cry?' And he said, 'Yes, yes, you should.' And I asked him, 'Am I, am I being rude?'"

I gape, "Really?!"

Maia nods, "I did, I did, and it wasn't, 'Should I be crying because it's sad?' it was, 'Am I being rude? Should I pretend I'm crying?' and he said, 'Yes, yes you should,' and so I let out this fake cry! I started to cry, you know, with everyone else, but I was faking the cry."

I peer at the screen closer to see if I missed something.

The corners of Maia's mouth fold upwards, "And then the next morning, at like 6:00 or 5:00 in the morning, we went to my father's coworker's house, where a lot of people who worked with my dad went because he had an actual house with a basement. So we went to his house and we stayed there in case there was another bombing. And everybody thought it would be a full-blown war. Luckily, it didn't turn out to be."

Maia tells me more about her experience—about sharing a bed between six people and about waking up with no breakfast and running into the basement to hide and about moving to Yugoslavia and living with her grandparents and about her parents separating. And all I can think of is the girl with snakes for legs and the single tear I think I saw Maia shed.

I return to the screen. Maia speaks, " . . . because Communism was falling in Yugoslavia. You know. It was right before the Balkan War and there was—"

"Maia," I say.

"—really big recession and no work."

I speak louder, "Maia."

"Uh?" Maia says. She cranes her neck to the side.

"Maia, did you cry?"

Her jaw shifts side to side, "What?"

"That little girl with snakes for legs. You were thinking about her. Did you cry?"

"Well everyone else was crying, there were enough people crying. I didn't have to cry because everyone—"

"No," I say. "Just now. When you were thinking of her. Did you cry?"

"It, it's not like that. I don't have to cry. There's enough crying without, without—"

"Just tell me." I glare at her, I raise my voice, "Just now. Did you cry just now?"

Maia's head quivers back and forth, "Rebecca, are you tired? You look upset. Maybe we should continue this tomorrow morning. It's late."

"No," I say and my fist descends against the side of my computer, "No. I want to know now. Did you cry? Did you cry about the little girl with snakes for legs?"

"I have to be up for work at 6:00 a.m. I'm going to sleep now. Good night," Maia says.

The connection cuts. The little green dot beside Maia's name disappears.

On June 26, a little after noon, I sit with Maia in the window of Niche Coffee and Tea on Queen West. Traffic sounds flow around us as the tall french doors swing in the breeze.

"By the way, I cried for real," Maia says.

I'm not sure what she means at first. She's been telling me about her new job at a women's group home.

"I said I faked crying. But I really cried." Maia's face pinches and her eyes mist. "I really cried about her, the girl."

I enunciate, as though it will help me remember, "Girl."

Maia whispers, "The girl with, with—"

"Oh," I say. "Oh!" I jump down from my stool and race to her side of the little table.

I throw my arms around her and press her face into my shoulder. "You don't need to. Don't say it. I'm sorry. I didn't mean to—"

Maia pushes my shoulders back with her palms. She peers into my eyes, purses her lips into a half-smile, and nudges me back to my seat.

"There's enough sadness in the world. I try to be happy," Maia smiles. "Anyway, at the group home, this one woman, she really cracks me up. She's stuck in a wheelchair but—"

Nap Time

Ken Levine

I lie on a blue gym mat. Sally lies next to me on her mat, and Adam lies next to her on his mat. Miss G stands by the front door and turns off the lights. I roll onto one side. I roll to the other.

I stare at Sally. I watch Sally's closed eyes. I turn over and see Jason's eyes shut. I peer at Amanda. Amanda closes her eyes and sucks on her thumb.

Miss G rustles papers. I flip my chin up and search for Miss G. She sits at her desk, brown hair in a bun, red glasses tilted down.

I scan for the clock. The little hand points to one, and the big hand points to two. The clock ticks, ticks, ticks, and I don't know how to tell time from this kind of clock, and I force my eyes shut and remember hiding in the bushes next to my grandparents' front door and how I surprise them every time I go to visit them in San Diego with my parents.

I remember asking Mommy, "Why do I have to go to daycare?"

"Because we are staying here for a couple of months. It will be fun! You will play with kids your own age."

"Why are we staying here so long?"

"Because I want to spend more time with my parents, honey."

I open my eyes and gaze out the window. The sun peeks through the shades. I imagine recess time and climbing up the wooden ladder and running, diving, and ducking to avoid tagging hands.

My legs shake against the ground.

I inch off my mat and tiptoe to Miss G's desk, "Miss G, I need to use the washroom."

Miss G sits up, "The what?"

My neck scrunches and I swallow, "I, I mean, the bathroom."

"It's naptime." Miss G points, "Go back to your mat."

I turn around, take a step, then twist back, "But Miss G, I really, really need to go."

Miss G nods to the empty blue mat, "You should have gone before naptime."

My feet drag past James and Ally, and I curl up back on my mat. I clench. I rock in place. I find the clock. The little hand points to the right. The big hand points to the right and down further than the little hand. I squeeze my eyes shut and wish I knew how to understand these clocks.

In Toronto I don't have naptime. In Toronto I don't have to say bathroom. In Toronto I don't have to sing God Bless America.

I wrap my arms around my stomach and hold tight, and I don't think I will make it until the end of nap time, and I don't know why the teacher won't let me go. And how can I nap if I have to go to the washroom?

I flip back to my side. My stomach turns circles and tightens. I make fists and I push my head into the mat.

Amanda whispers to Jessica, and Jessica giggles.

Miss G shoots up, "Keep quiet, girls. Keep those eyes closed!"

Miss G shifts her chair and it scratches against the white floor. I squiggle in place.

I squeeze my eyes, I squeeze my fists, I squeeze my shoulders, my stomach, my butt, my legs, and my toes. I squeeze everything until I shiver. What if I can't hold on, and Miss G sends me to the office and calls Mommy, and all the other kids find out and stare at me and point and laugh at me? I have to hold it in.

I can't. I can't hold on anymore. My body falls limp, my muscles release, and I wish, wish, wish that no one can hear. Or smell. Or see.

I scan the room. Miss G pushes up from her desk.

I press my eyes shut and slip a finger under my glasses to wipe the tears off my cheeks. I can sneak to the washroom. I can grab my backpack from the cubby and change myself, and no one will ever know.

Miss G's heels click across the tiled floor. "Naptime's over, boys and girls. Get your hats from your cubby and line up in front of me for recess."

Jason darts to his cubby. Amanda skips, Jessica twirls, and Adam stumbles to line up first in front of Miss G.

I grab the sides of my shorts. I press my legs together. I inch to my backpack. I clutch it under my arm and shuffle to the washroom. I slide into a stall and lock the door.

I unzip my backpack and dig to find the grocery bag of extra clothes Mommy always puts for me. I shift closer to the toilet. I sidle out of my shorts, I slip my underwear down, and I lift one foot out, then the other. I avoid the two, big plops of poo. I grab the underwear and tip the poops into the toilet. I wipe my bum.

I stuff the soiled underwear into the now empty bag, tie it, wrap it in a ball, and shove it to the bottom of my backpack. I put on fresh underwear and shorts, then slip back into my shoes. I scrub my hands ten seconds, like Mommy taught me, and dry them.

I ease out of the washroom. I stash my backpack in the cubby, grab my Toronto Blue Jays hat, and sneak to the back of the line.

Penance

Loredana Polidoro

G et out of the way, fatso." Joe Santoro body checks me as he leaves the classroom.

I glance at Ms. Copeland to see her reaction. She arranges her supplies on her desk, making sure not to look up.

I follow my Grade 8 classmates down the stairs and out the front doors, single file. We cross the playground that doubles as the church's parking lot beside our school. The church and school share the same name—Saint Rose of Lima. We shuffle towards the large, heavy wood doors. We stream into the church, shoulders slouched, heads down, hands clasped in front of our bodies.

I place my fingers in the holy water font as I enter the church. I sprinkle the water on my forehead, centre of my chest, and both of my shoulders in the sign of a cross. I peek up at the front of the church and study the large crucifix just above the priest's chair. The dark brown work depicts Jesus' body as it lies limp on the cross. The muscle and sinew on his emaciated body glisten in the lights placed directly above.

Two lines have formed in front of the confessionals. I notice Amanda at the end of one line and dash towards her. My sneakers squeak on the marble floor. Twenty-two pairs of eyes glare at me. My face burns. I feel red-faced and heavy.

I quicken my pace and join the line behind Amanda. I try to hide my obese body behind my petite Filipina friend. Amanda turns to me and smiles. I nod and try to ignore the others.

The line inches toward the confessional. One student exits, another enters. One by one we make our act of contrition.

I whisper to Amanda to wait for me in the pews at the front of the church. Amanda nods and trudges into the confessional. She slides the heavy maroon velvet curtain shut. The red bulb above the booth lights up.

The two-minute wait for my turn drags. I want to get a head start on recess.

The red light goes out. Amanda emerges, her hands clasped in prayer and her head down. She strolls toward the pews at the front of the church to say her penance.

I stumble into the confessional and heave onto the kneeler. The wood creaks under my weight. I lean my elbows on the armrest and clasp my hands together. I face the small, square, screened window that separates me from the priest. I bow my head and wait for the priest to reveal himself.

The screen slides open. My heart beats in my throat. The side of the priest's face appears through the lattice-print screen. He bows his head as my cue to confess my sins.

"Bless me father for I have sinned," I recite. "It has been three months since my last confession. These are my sins."

I rattle off a list of offences. I talked back to my parents. I said the Lord's name in vain. I hit my brother.

"For these and all my other sins, I am truly sorry." I conclude my role in the sacrament and anticipate my absolution.

I hold my breath as I wait for the priest's response.

"For your penance, my child," the priest begins, "I want you to lose weight."

I take a quick breath and hold it. Silence echoes in the small booth. My ears and face feel as though they have been set on fire. I squeeze my eyes shut and force back tears.

The priest raises his hand toward his head. "I absolve you of your sins in the name of the Father, the Son, and the Holy Spirit."

I bring my right hand to my forehead and, with him, make the sign of the cross. The screen shuts abruptly.

I push my weight forward and hoist upwards. I rub my eyes and nose on my sleeve and take a deep breath.

I exit the confessional, focus on my sneakers, and watch one foot move in front of the other towards the altar. I slide into the second row pew and settle next to Amanda.

"So what did you get?" Amanda asks. "Two Hail Mary's and an Our Father?" she guesses.

"Um, no," I respond.

Amanda crinkles her brows, "Then what did you get?"

"He told me to lose weight."

"Oh!"

Amanda and I linger and stare at our shoes.

"Let's get out of here," Amanda says.

I follow Amanda out of the pew and up the nave of the church.

As I approach the door to leave, I reach for the holy water font for my final blessing. I feel my fingertips touch the surface of the water. I start to dip my fingers, then yank my hand back towards me and shake away the drops. The water falls onto the cold marble floor, and my hand floats above. I wipe my hand dry on my thigh, and I walk out the door.

The Fishing Game

Deena Kara Shaffer

The inch-long, multi-coloured plastic fish of the Hasbro fishing game bob up and down as they turn. Bright pink, blue, and green jaws open wide and snap shut. They circle the battery-driven pond. Bubbi, my parents, and I sit in our living room. I kneel in front of the coffee table. Bubbi sits in the brown corduroy armchair opposite me and leans forward. We clutch our small fishing rods. Bubbi's hands, at eighty, appear wrinkled, spotted, and soft. I am four, and my hands look plump, pink, and smooth. Mum and Dad sip afternoon martinis and watch.

I swing my rod over the colourful jaws.

Bubbi reaches for a fishing pole. "Show me how to do it."

I roll my eyes. "Bubbi, you know how."

"Remind me. Show me again."

Bubbi grips her rod with its yellow ball at the end. The motorized disk rotates. Fish pop up with widened jaws that close tightly as they lower. Around and around the fish travel. I hover Bubbi's string an inch above and guide it into an open-mouthed fish.

Bubbi yanks the fish out, "Got it!"

"Hey! That doesn't count! Now you try. But you have to hold it by the rod."

"Wouldn't it be easier your way?" Bubbi says.

"Yeah, but I was showing you. You're supposed to hold it like a real fishing rod."

Bubbi takes the ball, places it in the gaping mouth of a fish and pulls, "Right, right."

I jump to my feet, "Bubbi! That makes it too easy!"

Bubbi snatches the fish, "Two, nothing."

"Bubbi! That's not fair!" I stamp my feet on the hardwood floor.

"I'm an old lady. A widow. You should be proud."

I bury my head in my hands, "Okay, but from now on, you have to do it for real."

Bubbi and I inch closer to the board. We eye the fish. Our gazes meet.

Mom calls Bubbi bosomy. I think of her as pillowy. Her once hourglass figure has become an ample bust perched on stick legs.

I snatch a pink fish and grin, "I got one!"

Bubbi groans.

We hover, gripping our fishing rods. The fish's jaws tease us as they pass by and seal shut before we can hook them.

Bubbi throws her rod to the floor, "Drat! I almost got that one! That one should count."

"It doesn't work like that," I say. "Keep trying."

I pick up Bubbi's fishing rod and hand it to her.

"But . . ."

"Just keep trying, Bubbi. You're still winning."

"Okaaay."

The yellow ball at the end of Bubbi's rod swings over the fish's mouths. My parents laugh.

I spin my fishing rod over the board, and plop it down. "I got another one! That's two all! Yes!"

"Sweetheart," Bubbi says, "what's that over there?" She motions her head to the left and cocks her chin up.

"What?" I stare where Bubbi points.

"Over there. Over there," Bubbi repeats.

"What is it? What do you—"

Bubbi throws her arms in the air, "I caught a red one!"

"Really? What? How did you do that so fast?"

Dad peeks over his martini, "Mum!"

"Whaaat?" Bubbi shrugs. "She didn't notice. Leave it."

I snap my head back and look at her, "Bubbi, were you cheating again?"

"What is this again business? I caught that fish fair and square!"

"Just like last week at checkers!"

"Forget all that. Keep playing, sweetheart. I'm winning."

Broken Telephone

Aya Nishiyama

Third place in hurdles. Second place in the hundred-meter race. First place in the inter-school relay. I situate the strips of blue, green, and red ribbon on my desk and race out of the classroom. Shouts and laughter fill the playground of Cleland Elementary School.

I recall this morning's track-and-field day. More than three hundred fifth-graders from Troy, Ohio, gathered at Robart Arena. My classmates swarmed around me. I couldn't understand what they said, but I imagined it was good. Instead of asking them to speak slower, I smiled. I wish everybody spoke Japanese.

I stretch my arms under the warm, early summer sunshine. The gentle breeze touches my exposed arms and legs. The scent of grass floats around.

I search for my playmate, Amy. I find her brownish blonde hair in the distance and rush over to her. She sits with Molly and Adam on the wooden frame of the sandbox. I grin.

"Hey guys, let's play . . . !" Amy yells to our other classmates who play on the slide in front of us.

I can't catch her last two words.

I hope Amy tells me what game we're playing.

"Count me in!" Shirley Sanders says. Her freckled face with squirrel-like eyes comes toward us. Other classmates join. Twelve of us make a circle and cross our legs on the grass. I still don't ask what game we're playing. I want to seem smart today.

"You can start, Luke!" Adam says.

"All ready," Luke ponders for a second. His eyes glint under his black-framed glasses. He puts his hands around his mouth, leans into Amy's ear, and whispers. Amy beams. She does the same action to the person next to her. Ah, I know what we're playing. It's Dengon Gemu, Broken Telephone. I sigh in relief, but then I stiffen again. What if I don't know all the words? What if I make a mistake? I'm the only one who makes stupid English mistakes. They'll know it was me.

My heart pounds. I shouldn't have joined this group. Adam reaches to Brian and whispers the phrase. Brian giggles. He puts his hands over my left ear. I blush. What if the phrase is too long? What if I can't catch his words? What if—

"Mr. Natta slips on a banana."

Phew. I know all the words. My shoulders relax. I put my hands around my mouth and whisper into Molly's ear. She chuckles and enunciates my words. The circle breaks into laughter. The first round ends.

"Let's change spots!" Shirley Sanders suggests. Everybody moves. I stay. Shirley Sanders sits next to me.

"I'll start!" Shirley Sanders shouts. She whispers into Molly's ear. Molly whispers into Amy's ear. Amy's eyebrows wrinkle. Amy whispers into Brian's ear. I wonder why Shirley Sanders sits next to me. She ignores me in class.

Brian whispers into Luke's ear. Luke whispers into Danny's ear. Oh God, please, I want an easy phrase. What if Shirley Sanders made a long, complex phrase? My heart pounds. Adam whispers into Becky's ear. Becky puts her hands over my ear. I sweat. What if, what if . . .

"Go back to your country."

My heart stops. Blood retreats from my forehead, my cheeks, and my neck. It retreats from my heart. I understand every word.

The green grass, the blue sky, the June sunshine, and the shouts of kids whirl before me. Without a word, I rise. I flee the circle.

"Aya, wait!" I hear Amy shout.

I sprint. The world blurs. Sound fades.

I melt into the wind.

Balls

Shoshana Green

I pat my hair, touch each earring, and press Elaine Burgess's doorbell. A shadow darkens the frosted front-door window. I smile over my shoulder and throw my mom a careless wave. Elaine opens the door, and I hear our Suburban rumble off down Cumberland Avenue.

"Come in!" Elaine says and leads me through her house.

Narrow stairs creak down to an L-shaped rumpus room. Wood panelling rises from plush crimson carpet. A sectional sofa hugs the corner.

Mrs. Wilson's sixth-grade class fills Elaine's basement. I imagine Mrs. Wilson at home, watching TV with Mr. Wilson.

Girls crowd the far wall, sneaking hair and makeup checks in the marbled mirror tiles. Some arrange themselves on the floor. Others attempt natural-looking standing poses. Carrie Olsen smoothes her mini-skirt, and I check mine. My heart pauses at the thought of exposing my underwear.

The boys sit in a group on the couch. The geeks jumble together, almost on top of each other, and leave extra room for Mark Thompson, Chad Edwards, and Shawn Reimer.

Mark, Chad, and Shawn debate Guns 'N' Roses versus Skid Row. An all-slow-dance mixed tape plays. I envision Elaine choosing each song, consulting her older sister, and planning the order.

At 7:45 Elaine's mother coughs a few times from the top stair. She comes down with a tray of hot pizza buns. She lays them on the table, smiles, and rushes back upstairs. The boys devour the pizza buns. Most of the girls stand back from the table. Elaine and Tara Bowman take turns nibbling the edges of a shared bun. I eat a whole one. It burns my mouth right behind my front teeth.

I stand beside Stacy Jones. We have been best friends for two months. I remember the first time Stacy called me.

"Is Shoshana there?" A familiar girl's voice came through the black telephone handset.

"This is Shoshana." I said.

"Hi, it's Stacy! Turn on CKOM! The Top 20 is on! They're about to play 'Angel of Harlem'!!"

"What's that?" I said.

"Oh my God. You don't know U2?!"

I paid $22—more than a month's allowance—for the Rattle 'n' Hum cassette. And I trained myself to say, "Me and Stacy are going to the mall, me and Stacy are going to a movie," instead of correcting her.

"I think we should play spin-the-bottle," Stacy says.

I squeeze my eyes shut and travel back to Stacy's birthday party last month. I feel the carpet of Stacy's basement under my spread fingers and see Jeremy Lee's round glasses glint as he darts across the circle and brushes his pinched lips near my ear.

"Um, yeah. Maybe," I say, opening my eyes.

"Let's go over there," Stacy says.

"Where?"

She nods in the direction of the guys, "There."

Elaine and Tara chat with some of the guys.

Stacy steps forward. I freeze, inhale, and rush to catch up with Stacy. We stand in front of Chad.

A curtain of brown hair conceals his eyes. He squints and arches his brows like Christian Slater. He sprawls on the floor in front of us, and his long legs stretch through tight black jeans. A lime green Chip & Pepper Wet Wear shirt hugs his chest and shoulders. One arm supports his head. His square jaw tilts upward.

"Hey, Chad," says Stacy.

"Hey, Stacy. What's up?"

Stacy plays football, real boy-football, with helmets and tackling. The guys talk to her all the time.

"You're kind of taking up a lot of space, you know." Stacy tilts her head and flicks her braid back over her shoulder.

"Yeah, well, it's going to waste otherwise."

"You're pretty vulnerable right here, you know," Stacy says and points to a spot in the middle of Chad's pants.

Chad smirks. My eyes risk one more second on his lips before widening to take in his face, hair, and the air around him. Hope tingles up my spine and desperation turns somersaults in my stomach.

Stacy says, "You know, Shoshana, you could kick him right in the balls right now if you wanted." My head jerks up. Did she just say 'balls'?

Stacy smiles and her tongue peeks out the side, "I dare you."

I gaze down at smirking Chad. Chad has called me fat, he's called me weird, he's called me prissy, and I have kicked boys in the balls before, in the lower grades, on the playground with my friend, Charity. And I never get dared to do things like this.

I eye Chad. Stacy raises her eyebrows and grins at me. I lift my foot, swing it back ten, twenty, thirty centimetres, and let go. My foot swoops forward, sinks into the cushion of Chad's crotch and pauses for two seconds, toe-deep. Chad's face creases like when he laughs or smells a fart. I step over him and walk to the snack table. Stacy stays beside Chad. Fear grips my throat and I don't look back at Stacy.

———

Stacy and I sit on the couch. Her Swatch reads 8:15. I stare at the cleared space in the middle of the room where nobody dances.

Someone says, "What's going on?"

"It's Chad," a girl answers.

"Is he crying?" another girl says.

Stacy stands up. Her long stride bridges the space between the couch and the crowd, "Shoshana kicked him in the balls."

"You dared me to!" I say.

"I was joking! You can't actually do that! Not when a guy's just lying there!"

"Do you want some ice?" Elaine says. She and Tara snicker.

I cower beneath teased and hairsprayed bangs and try to sink into the couch, away from the light and the stares of my classmates.

"Are you retarded? Like, literally?" Mark glares.

My eyes shift from his face to his shoulder to the wall.

"Seriously, Shoshana. You are a total idiot," says Shawn.

Stacy pulls me aside. She shakes her head and rolls her eyes, "That really wasn't smart."

I nod.

Chad hunches on the couch. Shawn hands him a Coke. Chad's limbs relax, but he keeps his head down and avoids eye contact.

The crowd disperses. The shy girls move back to the far wall. They whisper in twos and threes. I have given them a story.

"Chad. What do you want to hear?" Mark asks.

"Chili Peppers," Chad mutters.

Mother's Milk thrusts through wall-mounted speakers. I flush every time I see the cassette with the beautiful shirtless model cradling the band to her breasts. Heat rises in my chest. Tears flood my vision. My skull aches. And Stacy babbles about the boy who sells New York Fries at Midtown Mall.

Mrs. Viola

Candice Frederick

Mrs. Viola yells at our Grade 9 French class.

Mrs. Viola misplaces the chalk.

Mrs. Viola wears brown polyester pants on Mondays, Wednesdays, and Thursdays.

Notre Dame is an all-girls, Catholic high school near the Beaches in Toronto. We have nuns, but they no longer wear habits.

I choose the same seat every class.

Alisha sits in front of me.

Mrs. Viola faces us. Her large wooden desk blocks the front of the classroom.

"Want some?" Alisha applies pink gloss to her plump lips. She tilts the container in my direction.

"Um. No . . . but thanks," I say.

Alisha looks at me and shrugs. She pulls the gum from her mouth and sticks it under the lid of her desk.

Mrs. Viola turns back to the board. Mrs. Viola writes in her slanted scrawl. French verbs crowd the chalkboard: *Être. Aller. Avoir.* I count down the minutes until lunch. My stomach grumbles and my head aches.

Annette saunters in wearing our white uniform shirt, freshly starched, and perches on the seat next to mine. "Did I miss anything?" she asks.

She unrolls a red fruit roll-up. I eye it.

"Not yet," I say.

"Did you do all the homework?" Annette asks Alisha.

Alisha rolls her eyes, "No. She never checks anyways."

Alisha's purple-and-blue pleated skirt looks shorter today. The pin points up to indicate that she has a boyfriend. She likes to brag about how she met him in Trinidad.

Annette grabs my notebook and starts copying.

Mrs. Viola continues to write. She mumbles with her back to our class.

Our school has many smart girls and many pregnant girls. We go to mass every week. We stand in front of emaciated Jesus, nailed to the cross. We sing. We confess our sins. I tell the priest about the lies I tell my Mom, and I receive my penance of Hail Mary's. I chew the Body of Christ. I mumble words to some of the songs. I do not always know when to make the sign of the cross. I may be a bad Catholic.

Mrs. Viola never sends students to the office when our uniforms are too short or we wear the wrong shirt. Ms. Terry, the other French teacher, measures the length of each kilt with a ruler and knows which shirts aren't uniform.

Annette elbows me and jerks me out of a daydream. I notice Mrs. Viola's stare. My heart races. Am I in trouble? My armpits dampen.

A textbook crashes to the floor on the other side of the classroom. Mrs. Viola shifts her gaze to Kalika and her friends. They laugh. Mrs. Viola's eyes narrow but she says nothing.

"Who wants to read their homework?" she asks. No one raises a hand.

I avert my eyes to the dirty, grey classroom floor.

"Mrs. Viola would like someone to read their homework aloud," Mrs. Viola says and addresses the class in third-person. Her voice rises and tremors. Her hands tremble.

"Girls. Come on. Mrs. Viola is very displeased with this class."

Annette fidgets. She lowers her blonde head to the desk. Her shoulders shake and her mouth twitches.

I stiffen my body to avoid laughing. I avoid eye contact with Annette. I avoid eye contact with Mrs. Viola.

Mrs. Viola raises her voice more. Her face turns red.

Alisha pulls out the mirror she uses to apply her lip gloss. I see her tip it to the left. She catches a strong beam of sunlight. The light bounces off the window and into Mrs. Viola's eyes.

Mrs. Viola spreads her hands in front of her face and takes a step back. Her head bows.

We all freeze. We brace for our sentencing.

Alisha lowers the mirror, her brown eyes open wide.

Mrs. Viola's hands flop down to her sides. Her shoulders slouch. Her head bobs down and then back up. A single tear trails down her pale cheek. The bell rings and we rush out the door.

Annette hands me a bright package in the hallway. I rip it open. Why is she handing me a romance novel with Fabio, the long-haired soap star, on the cover?

"Like it?" Her blue eyes shine with eagerness.

"Thanks," I murmur. My face feels hot. My eyes dart across Fabio, and I forget about Mrs. Viola.

"You're blushing," Annette says.

"Seriously, Annette," Alisha says. She pats me on the back and smiles, "You might learn something."

Annette shakes her head at Alisha.

Mrs. Viola shuffles by our group, her chin pressed close to her chest.

Fabio might be good for Mrs. Viola too.

Ricky

Alesia Malec

I tiptoe down the second floor hallway. My heart races, my palms sweat, and I peek inside Mr. Welland's classroom, Homeroom 4B. Warren, Tina, Barry, and Lisa sit in a column of green desks by the windows. Warren folds his hands and rests them on his desk, Tina hunches over and writes a note, and Barry drums the wooden desktop with a pair of pencils. I stare at the empty seat at desk 1A. Ricky's desk. My shoulders roll down and my breath releases.

I skip to my locker at the back of the classroom, hang up my turquoise hoodie, and change into running shoes. I sit at desk 3C, near the middle of a centre column. I scan the timetable on the chalkboard: Language Arts, Math, Recess, Phys. Ed., Phys. Ed., Lunch Break. I hope Mum made macaroni and cheese.

Desks fill with my Grade 4 classmates. Conversations drift around the room. Some boys talk about Kenworth trucks and two girls giggle at a cute boy on a magazine cover. The room smells of chalk, graphite, and laundry soap. I lift the lid on my desk and peer into the cubby space. I unzip my pencil case and dig out a yellow pencil and my pink-and-blue eraser. I drop the desktop with a thud. The bell rings. The door closes. Desk 1A remains vacant.

"Good morning class!"

Eighteen voices chime, "Good morning, Mr. Welland."

Mr. Welland raises his hands, "Everyone stand up for the national anthem." Natasha leaves the room. She doesn't sing. I should ask her why she leaves every morning.

" . . . Oh Canada, we stand on guard . . . for . . . thee!"

Natasha returns. Desk legs scrape the floor and eighteen students sit.

I eye Mr. Welland. His smile comforts me and his blue eyes crinkle as he gathers the class in his gaze. He stands tall, broad-shouldered, and wears a light green dress shirt and dark trousers but no tie. I like his laugh and we hear it often. He teaches our class every subject except Science. In Phys. Ed., he races with the boys until they all grow tired.

A queue grows along the row of low shelves in front of the window. The pencil sharpener perched at the far end of a shelf endures our abuse. I grab my pencil. Crank, crank, crunch, crunch. I blow on the tip. A sparrow alights on the window ledge. We peer at each other for a second before it flits away to a willow tree. The caretaker rides a lawn mower around the schoolyard.

Mr. Welland grabs a book off his desk. "Okay, class, let's get your readers out. Who wants to start?"

All hands remain down. No one looks at Mr. Welland.

Mr. Welland moves to the centre of the room and stands in front of the chalkboard. Four rows of desks form a checkerboard in front of him. He chuckles and begins to read. His lyrical baritone washes over me. Each of us then reads a paragraph. Kristy sniffles and rubs her nose, Todd holds his book inches from his dark-rimmed glasses and squeaks out a few sentences, and Trevor's monotone encourages us to daydream. A symphony of turning pages marks our advancement through the chapter. Jan's curls catch flecks of sunlight as she bobs her head in time to her recitation. My index finger underlines each word as she reads. I'm next.

Knock, knock, knock. Book spines crack. Jodie and Tina whisper and giggle.

"Mr. Welland, Ricky is a bit late," whispers the secretary.

Ricky darts past the secretary and throws himself into his seat. A red, Jaws T-shirt drapes his thin frame, his dusty hair stands on end, and the hems of his jeans don't meet his shoes. Ricky rummages inside his desk, pulls out every book, and slams them down one by one. His dirt-filled fingernails flip open a math book. My heart pounds.

"Thanks, Miss Walters. We'd just got started." Mr. Welland's smile doesn't reach his eyes.

A low growl escapes Ricky's throat as he turns to Warren, "What are you guys doing? Which book do I need?"

Warren leans over and points. Ricky flicks Warren's hand away.

"One day when errb'dy—inda housedd sumpin' azzorbin' tadoo . . . ."

Ricky's words fire in rapid succession. Lisa flinches, and it spreads to Tina and Jodie. My shoulders reach for my ears.

Mr. Welland interrupts. "Thank you, Ricky. Jan, would you mind going again?"

Ricky yells, "I wasn't finished!"

Mr. Welland strolls to the front of the room. His light brown hair has fallen over his forehead.

He plants his feet and towers over Ricky, "We are all taking turns. It's Jan's turn. You have to wait."

Ricky glares at Mr. Welland and then at Jan. Jan turns away. I study my reader.

"I'm not waiting. Everyone else can wait." Ricky sneers.

Mark taps his knee with an eraser.

Mr. Welland's smile vanishes. "Ricky, you know we take turns. It is not your turn."

SCREEEECH! The hinges on Desk 1A wrench apart and the desktop separates from the cubby-space below. Splinters frame empty screw holes on the underside of the wooden slab. Ricky grips the edges of the slab. His face turns purple, his black eyes scan the classroom, and he reveals his teeth. His arms thrust forward. SMASH! The broken desktop sails over Mr. Welland's chair and clangs to the floor. Ricky races to the door. Mr. Welland darts past Kristy and Todd. SLAM! The door rattles and the floor shakes. Shoes squeak on the floor, an eraser bounces on a desk, and I hear Jan breathe in and out.

Mr. Welland's left arm circles Ricky's waist. Ricky thrashes and roars. Mr. Welland steps to the classroom door, turns the doorknob, pushes the door away from him, and strides out the door, Ricky on his hip.

My lips press into a line. I swallow and close my reader.

Eighteen minds wait.

All the Jokes in Egypt

Heba Elsherief

P rofessor Campbell asks us how we would describe love.
"Imagine," he says, "if you have to teach someone, an alien
or something not human or maybe something human that doesn't
know what love is—someone who has never experienced what
love is—what the concept of love means."

Students offer up ideas of how love makes you feel. I remain
quiet and unsure. Does he want us to explain what love means or
how it makes people feel?

Jane Grace, the Canadian literature expert, sits in her wheelchair at the front of the class. She says, "I might tell them that love
is a stone angel that speaks to you even as it is physically unable to
manifest its voice, even as stone is unable to speak."

Professor Campbell hesitates for a few seconds. He takes off
his glasses, puts them back on again. He smiles and nods. "I love
that," he says and stresses the word 'love' in his comment. He
launches into a lecture about metaphors and concepts of sweetness
and bitterness and stoney-ness and love. I take notes on Professor
Campbell's words, snippets here and there, like salt sprinkled
from a shaker on something without flavour. I pen bullet points in

my notebook, 'stronger than similes, limitations of metaphor, assumptions, conflicts, and explicitness.' Professor Campbell starts into the history of metaphor in poetic expression. I doodle in the margins of my notebook, and I wonder how I would describe the concept of love. A moment that happened years ago comes to my mind.

———

"So, one night, they gathered all the jokes in Egypt and threw them in the ocean. When they woke up in the morning—"

Uncle Mahmood stops. I recognize his technique, the technique of a master. Everyone loves it. Everyone loves him because he makes them laugh. He scans the room and makes eye contact with each member of his audience. I am first, closest to him. I sit on the couch with ornate upholstery. My cousin, Iman, sits beside me.

Across from Uncle Mahmood, my father and brother lie on a mattress on the floor. They recline opposite each other and their elbows meet in the middle. They've eaten too much of Aunt Faiza's late lunch of grilled chicken, flavoured with lemon zest and cumin, roasted potatoes, and macaroni with béchamel butter cream sauce. They've also drunk too much of her freshly squeezed mango juice, not knowing like I did that she watered it down when she heard that her twin sons, Ayman and Ashraf, were bringing their work friend, Ahmed, for lunch. The three of them complete Uncle Mahmood's audience.

My twin cousins sit on the loveseat, and Ahmed sits in the corner chair by himself. Ahmed wears a silver and topaz ring on his pinky. He sips mango juice, and the topaz catches a beam of sunlight that seeps through the shutters. His curls hang from his head and frame his face. I follow my Uncle Mahmood's gaze as it takes in the room.

————

"His curls were nice," I jot in the margin of my notebook. It's a wonder I didn't focus on Ahmed more that day, during my uncle's joke. I wonder where Ahmed is now. I didn't see him again. It would be weird to ask my cousins.

Professor Campbell speaks, "In his seminal text, Metaphors We Live By, Lakoff argues that—"

I shake my head and focus on the professor. I should know Lakoff. I've studied Lakoff's concepts in other courses. Our small lecture hall feels stuffy. The back of Jane Grace's wheelchair catches my focus. I stare at its bulging back pocket. I cannot figure out what it contains. The guy next to me sips from a Starbucks cup, and the smell of pumpkin spice wafts toward me. I wrinkle my nose.

"Lakoff's ideas revolutionized the way people think about metaphors," our professor continues. His eyes focus on the PowerPoint slide behind him. "To be competent in conceptual metaphors is to be—"

I've lost track of my thoughts and have given up on what Professor Campbell says. I scribble, 'Metaphors We Live By,' and add five exclamation marks to help me remember. My eyes fall on what looks like an unsolvable mathematical equation at the top of my notebook: Love? What it Means >vs< How it Feels. What did I mean?

————

My eyes follow Uncle Mahmood as he surveys the room and continues his joke.

He says, "So one night, they gathered all the jokes in Egypt and threw them in the ocean. When they woke up in the morning . . . "

I notice my Aunt Faiza, standing in the corner behind the loveseat. Wrinkles crease her face like lines on a map, and dark circles eclipse the wrinkles around her eyes. She wears an apron covered with stains from lunch. Aunt Faiza stares at Uncle Mahmood, and I think he must be staring at her too, but when I turn to him, he's missing the look she gives him. I've observed the look second-hand, and it gives me goosebumps.

My cousins laugh and catch every word of Uncle Mahmood's joke. Aunt Faiza watches Uncle Mahmood, he watches everyone else, and I watch Aunt Faiza. I see love in her gaze.

Uncle Mahmood's voice booms with the punchline, " . . . when they woke up in the morning, they found all the fish were laughing!"

When It Happens

Rebecca Brenner

My mom and I travel to Dundas, Ontario the day it happens. My dad stays home.

My trio rehearses at my violin teacher, Marla's, house for an upcoming competition. We practice Shostakovich's 4th Piano Trio. The three of us have played together for around a year. I play violin. Thomas plays cello. Aaron plays piano.

We complete the first bar before Marla presses her fingers into her forehead and then points them at me. "Rebecca!" she says, "You didn't cue clearly enough!" She heaves herself out of the pink-striped armchair and thrusts her baton at me.

"Okay everyone, start at the beginning. And, Rebecca," her mouth puckers. "Sniff! Don't snnnniiiiiffff."

I sit with my violin beneath my chin and stare at the portrait of young Marla in a puffy blue gown. Thomas hunches over his cello, his right arm limp against the strings. Aaron flexes his nostrils at me.

Marla rolls her eyes, "What are you waiting for?!"

I jerk myself up straight, take a sharp intake of breath as I raise my violin, make eye contact with both guys, and lower my violin for the first note. My heart drums between my ribs and my ears curl inward. I wait for Marla's scream.

The atonal melodies wrap me in their folds. I try to fit five beats where four should go and I forget about Marla. I repeat the melody, pass it to Thomas, sink into the background, and become small enough to fit inside a grace note. The music sinks and swells and terrifies and mollifies and then we begin the final ascent to the discordant finale. I picture the Siberian wasteland—the flat, the cold, the desolation—and my nose prickles with emotion. The piano rumbles below as I join Thomas in the high notes and we press our bows into high strings with all our strength and the tension builds into a taut rope of chords and the music slows and strangles us, then faster, with more force, stronger and more frenetic.

We sink back in our seats. Marla grins, "Bravo, bravo!"

I glide to my violin case in a daze, settle my violin in its hand-painted silk drawstring bag and lay the two velvet cloths on top. I unwind the mother-of-pearl screw at the end of the frog and position my bow opposite the violin. I zip the two sides of the case, set it by the front door, and hurry through the house to the back-yard. I imagine lunch waiting for us there. The plate of cut tropical fruit my mom brought, the bowl of Hungarian, cold cherry soup that Marla made, Erica's homemade Nanaimo bars, and samosas with tamarind sauce—fresh from Little India.

I beat the boys onto the patio. I tiptoe over the screen door ledge and peek around the muscat grape vine that loops around the patio trellis. "Ta–daaaa!" I burst through. "We're done!"

Erica leans over the grass, and Lisa flaps her arms by her sides. My mom lies on the grass, splayed like a starfish.

"Mom! Mom!" I cry. What's wrong with my mom? What happened to her? Is she going to be okay? Can she move?

I scream as I streak toward her, "Mom!"

She doesn't move.

"Mommy! Mommy! Moooommy!"

I throw myself down beside her, but she remains unmoving. She does not even open an eye. My mouth drops open, my eyes blur. I peer up at Erica and Lisa.

"House . . . " Erica murmurs.

"I . . . I don't care what happened in the house. Who cares about the rehearsal? Stupid stupid rehearsal. Wh—wh–what happened to my moooommy?" I fling myself on the grass by my mom and rest my cheek against hers. I cradle her head in my arms, thread my fingers through her hair, and try to shut out the thought of a world without her that keeps seeping into my conscious.

"Honey?" breathes a muffled voice in my ear. Hot air brushes my cheek.

I sit up, "Mom?! Mom, you're okay?!" I bend down to see her better, "Oh my god, Mom. What, what happened? Mommy, are you okay?"

She opens her eyes halfway. Her lips part, only in the middle.

"Mom!" I say.

Her lips seal back up, "Mom! Tell me what happened! Are you okay? Tell me! What happened?!!"

I look up, "Lisa? Erica? What's going on?"

They gaze back at me. Erica wrinkles her brow, scratches her neck.

"What happened?" I search them. "What's going on?"

Lisa peeks behind her and trembles. I realize that Thomas, Aaron, and Marla have come outside. Everyone stands, mute. Does anyone even know?

I turn back to my mom, forehead creased, pleading.

"Our house," she says. "Gone."

"What, Mom? What happened in the house? What's gone?"

Her upper lip curls back, her nose wrinkles on both sides. I know that look. What am I missing?

"Our house is gone," Mom says.

She hoists herself up, and her voice crescendos, "Our house. Our home. The house we live in. Gone. No more. Everything gone."

"What do you mean? What do you mean our house is gone? Where did it go?" I laugh in a high pitched whine, "We—we're going home after lunch!"

My mom's face blanches, "Our house is gone."

She collapses back to the ground. I force out another laugh and feel my upper cheeks begin to burn.

"Fire," Mom says.

"Fire? What?"

My mom gestures upwards with both hands, "Our house, whoosh—"

I can almost see the flames rise, the smoke travel through our home. I comb my hair back from my eyes and keep my hand there, holding on, "You mean our house? In flames?"

"Nothing left. All gone."

My childhood home. We drove away three hours ago. I think of my bedroom, how I left it this morning. The zebra-patterned quilt crumpled at the foot of my bed, my journal and green gel pen tucked beneath. My wooden jewelry chest on my pillow, top drawer open, and Bubbie's wedding ring nestled in the faded velvet. My favourite Calvin Klein jeans, cast aside in favour of this new mini-skirt I wear. My JVC CD player/radio, its blue light twinkling with Gil Shaham Devil's Dance still playing on loop. The little desk I begged my parents for and finally got a month ago. And my dolls. Molly and Candy, Anne and Moonflower.

I think of my bathroom painted with seahorses, and my parents' bedroom with the walk-in closet full of silk scarves, and the enormous white marble ensuite with the bathtub I used to get lollipops for using when I was too young to like being clean. I think of the long hallway that we only recently began to fill with framed artwork, and the stairs I used to thunder down to reach the first floor as fast as possible, and the maroon living room, and the dining room where I said my first word, "tickle," to our dog, Chelsea. I remember the kitchen with its falling-apart wicker armchairs, and the back deck where I read Pride and Prejudice for the first time.

I remember crawling up the stairs to our third floor when stairs were still something unexpected and wonderful and tracing my fingers over the paint splotches, spilled on those stairs before I was born, one shaped like a sparrow, the other like a crescent moon.

I think of our redecorated third floor, with tan leather couches and a real Persian rug and a wraparound desk for my dad. My dad. My dad is at home. Our house burnt to the ground and Dad is in the house.

My mom sits up. She studies me, "Honey?"

"Mom. Dad," I say. "Fire. House?"

Mom twists her jaw, her eyes blank, "Honey?"

"Dad."

Her face reshapes, "Oh, he's fine. He got out okay."

I lie back on the grass. My chest feels hollow, like a wooden spoon tunnelled deep inside and scooped out all the care. My muscles tense and then loosen. My fingers uncurl, my heartbeat settles, my mind decompresses. I focus on the sky, how blue, how vast, and how far away. The sun sits almost overhead and presses warmth into my pupils. It erases all but a ring of gold on the edge of my vision. The ring expands into a flaming orb, and I flow with the flame's undulations, gold, then grey, grey, then gold. First here, then there, here, and then gone.

Five Reasons

Dani Buchner

My phone buzzes.

"Rob?? What's up?"

My brother, Rob, and I never talk on the phone.

"Oh hey, Dani, I just got off the phone with Jim. He's going to call you. He sounds really fucked up."

"Yeah, well, we already knew that, didn't we?"

Jamie, Sarah, Cynthia, and Cole stare at me as I hop off of Jamie's single bed and leave her dorm room. I mouth the word *sorry* as I excuse myself and cross the hall to my own room.

"Just prepare yourself. He's been messaging me every day asking how to get you back."

I push a box of Jim's sweaters and socks out of the way as I enter my room. I close the door and plunk myself on my bed.

"Rob, trust me. That is so not going to happen. First of all, he cheated on me. Then, I found out through Facebook. Oh, and then after I dumped him, he starts writing me songs and sending them to Alannah?! I told her to delete him from MSN and she thinks I'm mean."

Alannah, my youngest sister, is in Grade 7.

"Yeah . . . I know it's weird. Anyways, I just wanted to let you know he's calling. Let me know how it goes."

"'Kay. Thanks, Rob. I will."

I stare at the wall next to my bed. White brick appears in the gaps of my photo collage where I have ripped off the photos of Jim and me. I pick at the pieces of sticky tac that once held them.

I fling pieces of sticky tac across the room and watch them hit the large, dirty, fingerprinted window above my desk.

My phone lights up before it starts to ring.

"Hey," I answer.

"Hi," Jim says.

"What do you want?"

"Listen," Jim says, "I know you hate me. I'm not going to try to get back together with you or anything. I just really need to talk to you."

"Why? I've already heard everything you have to say from my younger siblings. Which, by the way, is weirding everyone out. You need to stop doing that. Especially Alannah. Stop sending her your songs."

"I just need to talk to you. Can I come over?"

"You are talking to me. You can say it now."

"No, I need to see you. I went to the doctor today, and I have some things I need to tell you. Can I please just come over? I need to see you face to face. It's really important."

I cringe at the word *doctor*.

"Fine. Just tell me when you're here. I'll let you in."

I watch twenty minutes pass on the screen of my phone.

Jim knocks at my dorm window. His knocks trigger nausea. I glare at the floor as I head down the hallway to let him in.

Bags hang under Jim's eyes. Grey wrinkles crease his pale forehead. Tears well in his bloodshot eyes. His clothes hang off his frail body.

The hallway light buzzes. Chatter and laughter escape from Jamie's room. My eyes lock on the floor as Jim and I head back to my room.

"Listen," Jim says, "I don't want to ask too much. But I just really need a hug. Can I have one of those?"

"No."

Jim slumps onto my bed. I perch on my desk chair.

Outside my window other students laugh, sing, and yell as they head out to the bars.

"So, what do you so desperately need to tell me?" I ask.

"I . . . I was out with Nathan the other day, and I fainted. He took me to the hospital. I was there overnight. They did a bunch of tests on me."

"What were they testing for?"

"Well, because I was, like, in really bad shape when I got there. So they did all these tests on, like, my organs and stuff. You have to promise me you won't tell anyone what I'm about to tell you."

"Okay."

"Well, it turns out I have a rare, incurable organ disease. My organs are aging and deteriorating at an abnormally high rate. By the time I'm thirty, I'll have the organs of a hundred-year-old. Doctors don't think I will live much past thirty."

A rush of adrenaline makes me dizzy. I grip the side of my desk with my sweaty hand.

"What's it called?"

"It's so rare, they don't even have a name for it."

My eyebrows wrinkle, "So they can diagnose you with something there isn't even a name for?"

"Well I mean there is a name for it, but I don't remember."

"Oh."

"Please don't tell anyone. You are the only person I trust. You're the only one I can tell."

"What about your parents? You're only seventeen. Don't they have to know?"

"No, I guess not."

"What about Nathan? Didn't he take you to the hospital?"

"Oh yeah, they told Nate. So they didn't have to tell my parents because they told him instead."

"Okay . . . that doesn't really make sense."

"I don't know, my thoughts are just so cloudy right now."

I pass some Kleenex to Jim. He wipes his wet face.

"I just can't remember things straight. I have depression. But I can't take the medication for it because it messes up my brain, and I can't remember things anymore. Actually, I don't even remember cheating on you because of it. I have, like, permanent memory damage."

I stare at Jim, "That doesn't erase it."

"I know," he says.

Jim examines his wad of Kleenex. He crumples it into a tighter ball. "Well, the reason I had to have so many tests when I fainted is because a couple months ago the doctors told me I have lung cancer."

"Lung cancer? When did you find that out?"

"Like, December. That's why I started acting so weird. It wasn't drugs."

My eyes narrow.

Jim continues, "The doctors told me I didn't have much longer to live. I thought I was dying. That's why I cheated on you. I thought I was going to die anyways."

"You cheated on me because you have lung cancer?"

"Well, I don't actually have lung cancer. I went to two doctors, and they both said I had lung cancer. But I didn't believe them. I finally went to a third a few weeks ago, and I found out I don't actually have lung cancer."

"How did two doctors misdiagnose lung cancer?"

"I don't know. So annoying. But I thought I was dying. That's why I cheated on you."

Jim lowers his head. His fingers twist my bed sheets. His feet tap on the floor beneath my bed.

"I had a heart attack last week. Actually, two," Jim looks up at me.

"You had two heart attacks?"

"Yeah."

"And a rare incurable organ disease, possible lung cancer, depression, and a permanently damaged memory?"

Jim nods, hangs his head, and sniffles.

I hear Lauren, the girl next door, in our shared washroom. The sound of running water fills my dorm room.

"You are really skinny," I tell Jim.

"Yeah, that's because of my stomach ulcer."

"You have a stomach ulcer, too?"

Jim nods, "I haven't been able to eat in weeks."

My eyes trail up and down Jim's skinny body. His hands tap on his knees.

"Well, I don't really know what you want me to do or say."

Jim sighs, "Can I have a hug? I'm not asking you to get back together or anything, I promise. It wouldn't even be worth it now, knowing I'm not going to live past thirty. I'm not asking for you back. You're just the only person I can talk to. I just really need a hug right now."

Jim slips off my bed. I stand up, walk a step closer, and arrange my arms around him. I pat his back with my hand. He sobs into my shoulder. I turn away. He smells like soap, mouthwash, and marijuana.

"I guess I'll just go now," Jim says. He walks to my door and picks up his box of things.

"Okay," I say, "I hope everything works out for you . . . "

I close the door when Jim leaves. I watch through the peephole until he has crossed the auto-locked main doors. I stare at the bed where he sat and my hands shake. I close the curtain of the window above my desk.

Kaya

Aya Nishiyama

I click the green phone button on my MacBook screen. Kaya's pale face with black-framed glasses appears.

Kaya yawns and drawls, "Good morning. Do I have to turn on the video?"

"It's nice if you have it on. I can see your face," I say.

Her bob dangles to her shoulders. She munches a rice cake for her late Saturday breakfast.

Kaya lives in Yamaguchi, Japan, with her Brazilian boyfriend. We've been friends since our teenage years. In this Skype interview, Kaya unfolds her love stories, with boyfriends and girlfriends.

———

"When did you realize you're bisexual?" I say.

"Well, it was in Grade 6. Three boys bullied me at that time. They threw things at me and talked behind my back. They did cruel and violent things, like stoning a crow and putting the dead body into somebody's cubby. I guess they released their stress from entrance exams by bullying other classmates. I hated boys because of them.

"There was one girl who protected me from these boys. Her name was Yumi. She had a strong spirit and fought back against the boys. Yumi became my first love. I didn't tell her my feelings, though. One day, Yumi became the target. She cried so hard that our homeroom teacher had to call the boys' parents. The bullying ceased after the call."

Kaya bites off a piece of rice cake and scratches her neck. I ask her if she had a girlfriend in junior high school.

"In Grade 8, I fell in love with Minami, a girl in soccer club. I had to catch up with other team members because I joined the club a year after everybody else. So, during the winter break, I went to practice an hour earlier than the other members. Somehow, Minami was always there, in the soccer club meeting room. Minami and I chit-chatted there, instead of doing practice. We held hands and touched each other. That's all we did. We were still kids. But Minami was straight. Before entering Grade 9, Minami said, 'I can't go out with a girl. I can't do it.' That's how our relationship ended."

"Okay. Um, who was next?"

"Kozue. We didn't talk in school, but we became intimate through Yahoo Messenger in Grade 9. I chatted with her at night. When we went online, we could say anything, unlike in-person conversations. I wrote, 'I love you.' Kozue took it as a joke. Nothing happened for about a year."

I watch Kaya's face and wait for her to continue.

Kaya says, "I talked to Kozue face-to-face in Grade 10, during our spring retreat camp. She shared her family matters with me. I listened to Kozue's story. The next morning, she said she felt better because she shared her story. Kozue felt closer to me after that, but we didn't talk at school. We got passionate online. During the summer break, she came to my house. We touched. We kissed. By the end of the summer, we had sex."

"Didn't any of your family members notice your relationship with Kozue?" I ask.

"I thought they didn't know, but they did. Kozue and I visited each others' houses so often during the weekends and school breaks that my mom started to suspect our relationship. My mom read the text messages between Kozue and me, secretly. Mom said nothing. During spring break, I invited Kozue over to my house. Mom asked me, 'You're going out with Kozue, aren't you?' I told her, 'No I'm not!' But, one day, I witnessed my mom reading the messages. I thought, 'Oh shit! She does know about our relationship!'

"I stopped inviting Kozue over to my house. Instead, we met at her house. She loved me and was passionate about me, but she was embarrassed to tell anyone that she went out with a girl. She feared that her parents might find out about our relationship, and she became anxious, gloomy, and depressed.

"One day, Kozue told me, 'My parents say they're going to take me to a mental hospital.' I replied, 'Perhaps I should stop going to your house so often?' I visited her less.

"My parents asked me if I broke up with her. I told them, 'No, but her parents said they'll bring Kozue to a mental hospital, so I'm not visiting her as often.'

"My parents seemed shocked. They couldn't believe that I would still go out with Kozue despite her depression. My mom called Kozue's parents. They told my mom that I was the cause of Kozue's depression. Soon after the call, Kozue said she wanted to break up. So we broke up at the end of Grade 10."

"Did you have another girlfriend after Kozue?" I say.

"I did, but, before that, I had a boyfriend in Grade 11. I went out with him because I thought I could forget about Kozue. We broke up by the end of the school year, though. My next girlfriend, Nana, became my classmate in Grade 12. I didn't know her until then. At the beginning of the school year in April, Nana texted me frequently, but we didn't talk in school. In May, she wrote, 'You like girls, don't you?' I was stunned. I had never told anyone about my bisexuality. I trusted that Nana would keep my secret, so I replied, 'Yes.'

"Nana wrote back, 'Then will you go out with me?' I freaked out! I barely knew her! I had no idea why she liked me, so I asked her. She replied, 'I don't know. I can't explain. But I fell in love with you the first time I saw you.' Startled, I texted back, 'Thanks, but sorry, I don't know you that well. I think we need to know more about each other before we start dating.' I still liked Kozue then.

"Later that month, I learned that Nana had a boyfriend. I questioned her about it, and she said yes, but she broke up with her boyfriend immediately after. Our unclear relationship continued for four months. Nana studied for the university entrance exams during the summer break, so we didn't see or text each other for a while.

"In early September, Nana talked to me in school and said, 'I didn't see you during the summer break. I missed you.' I was shocked that she still liked me. I told her, 'You must study. It's not good timing for you to go out with anyone.' Nana said, 'No, that's not true. It's stressful to study all day long, every day. I need someone who supports me.' I accepted her love. We went out, but we only met at school.

"In February, I asked Nana if she wanted to come to my house. She said yes. We made love in my room. After graduation, we didn't see each other as often. Our relationship came to a natural end because I was busy with a part-time job, driving school, and studying and fencing at Hondo University. I hear that Nana has had a boyfriend for six years now. It seems I was her only girlfriend."

"Did you have another girlfriend or a boyfriend in university?" I say.

"I had two boyfriends. The first one didn't last very long. The second relationship had to break up because I applied for a one-year exchange program to Seiko University in Saitama."

"What made you decide to go to Seiko University?"

"Oh, I wasn't satisfied with the classes provided at Hondo University. Also, I wanted to meet new people, someone like me. I wanted to broaden my perspective. That's why I joined the LGBTQ student group, 'Rainbow Seiko.'"

"What did Rainbow Seiko do?"

"Some people did promotions—for example, creating short clips and showing them at the Seiko Festival. Others simply hung out with other members. It wasn't that different from other student groups. I usually attended the weekly lesbian meetings."

"I thought you identify yourself as bisexual. What made you join the lesbian gatherings?"

"I don't mind being called lesbian or bisexual. I thought I was eligible because I didn't have gender identity disorder. I attended the meetings to look for a girlfriend. And I heard many personal stories at Rainbow Seiko gatherings. I remember one from a transgendered girl. She had a girlish face, but she sounded like a guy and had a masculine body. She had no boobs. I thought it was rude to ask 'Which sexuality are you?' So, instead, I asked, 'What is your sexual orientation?' She replied, 'I'm not sure.' She told me that she had felt like a male from childhood, so, without hesitation, she started hormone treatment from an early age. But, just before her lower body operation, she stopped and wondered if she really wanted to be a male. She suddenly felt uneasy about changing her body. She decided the issue was not in her sexual orientation but in a world that requires heterosexuality.

"I remember her saying, 'Why do I have to decide my sexuality?'"

I stop, ponder, and ask Kaya, "How do you define your sexual orientation?"

"I don't know. I really don't know. When I was in Rainbow Seiko, I felt comfortable being viewed as a guy, and I was more attracted to girls. I thought of hormone treatment, half jokingly and half seriously. I didn't do it because of the physical and financial load. Now I identify myself as 'Bisexual FtX.'"

"What does that mean?"

"I can love both females and males. That's what bisexual means. The FtX part means 'Female to X.' I was born female, but I feel uncomfortable when people treat me as a girl. But it doesn't mean that I want to be a guy, and I hesitate to change my body. I can't define my sexual perception. That's what the 'X' means."

"What was good and what was bad about being involved in Rainbow Seiko?"

"Well, before I joined Rainbow Seiko, I thought I was crazy. But I wasn't. Nobody hid their sexual orientation in Rainbow Seiko. That's why I disclosed my bisexuality on Facebook."

I remember Kaya's confession on Facebook. She posted that she had a girlfriend and that she enjoyed being around the people in Rainbow Seiko.

"That was the good thing. The bad thing was . . . I was naive. There were people who were against homosexuality outside of Rainbow Seiko. Some friends didn't accept my coming out. They showed troubled expressions when I met them. Some stopped being my friends."

Kaya sighs and turns her gaze toward a piece of rice cake.

Copies

Keith Brown

Ellen Sanders tips her glasses down the bridge of her nose. Her eyes narrow into their hollow sockets and form a swath of wrinkles. I sink into my chair and dodge her unflinching gaze.

"Let me be frank with you," she says.

Her words sound measured and timed.

"The handwriting of your Final Exam is terrible. I could barely even read it. Chicken scratches all over."

She waves her hands around and then drops them on the hard wood desk. The whole weight of her body caves into the desk. Thirty years of teaching fall, exhausted and irritable, on that plain, dry surface.

This is my first year in university as an undergrad at York. The course is a mandatory social studies class, with an emphasis on social philosophy from Plato up to the present. I somehow imagined the meeting would be something more dignified: an oak-covered office with plush chairs, for instance. A celebratory mood, and something to tell me I passed a hurdle. At least there should have been a real plant instead of a plastic one held up by a straw and a fistful of aquarium rocks.

Boxes of papers line the cramped, untidy room.

Ellen leans forward into the burgundy folds of her sweater, "Tell me the truth." She sticks her index finger into my crumpled exam and with her thick New York accent says, "Were you nervous when you wrote this?"

"Um, I—" I gulp.

"Look, if you have chronically bad handwriting, you'd better be careful." She leans over even closer, as though to confer a nasty secret that only she and a few others know, "Some professors will dock marks for this kind of thing. I am just warning you, you know. They won't see what you can do."

"Yeah, yeah, " I say.

My lips stammer. My throat itches. I see myself from the vantage point of a spider in the corner of the ceiling: a small, thin, shrinking wisp of a boy, barely out of his teens, ninety odd pounds of awkward eagerness.

Ellen sighs, "Take this home with you and give me a clean, typed copy of your answers. Whoo boy." She rolls her eyes, "I don't do this with everyone, you know, but you're a good student. I'll cut you some slack. You have a weekend to do this and no more."

Ellen gets up from her chair, "Mail the original and typed version back to me afterward." She bends over to her next box of papers to resume her marking.

I walk out into the hall, and feel the weight of my steps drag down the stairwell. I am lucky. I wonder if she would bother checking to see if I changed my answers. It isn't likely that I would find something new to add to them anyway. And, like she said, I am a 'good' student. It wouldn't be in character if I tried to write it differently.

I sit down at my 1990, model T computer and type out the answers. I copy myself. Line by line, word by word, I trace the same paths that I traced before. One question asks me to compare Plato and Aristotle's ideas about politics. I write about Plato and his eternal ideas. I compare his utopian vision of the state with Aristotle's realist view of how societies actually evolved. I think about Aristotle's imitative view of art. Aristotle was surely a realist because he talks about art copying other things two or three times removed from the natural world. He was quite the pragmatic, come to think of it.

My basement apartment lies cold and quiet. It feels different than the hot exam centre, surrounded by fellow nervous folk. None of those students seemed to have issues with handwriting, choosing clothes, or walking down stairs without tripping. When I walked out, my hand felt sore and blue from all the ink I smeared. The weight of history from Plato to the present day blemished my hand, making me unable to form letters, let alone eat or comb my hair.

I have no way to print my typed exam. The school printing centre is closed on weekends. Besides that, my computer is old; the kind that uses dot matrix printers. I decide I will have to upgrade my computer when I have the money and wonder who would hire someone who spent four years writing footnotes to Plato and Aristotle. In the meantime, I have to ask my friend Khalid to print the exam for me.

Khalid is a year younger than me and in his final year of high school. He has dreams of becoming a computer programmer and making a whole lot of money at IBM or Silicon Valley. And he has all the latest technology. He answers my call from the Volvo that his dad lends him on weekends. He mentions that he is going to a sports store to find protein supplements. Recently, Khalid started going to the gym so that he could build up muscles. He claims that this is the sure and only way to attract girls.

"Face it," he tells me over the phone, "you and I are hard to want. Who the hell is going to love us unless we put on the muscle? That's what girls want. Am I right?"

"Yeah. I guess so," I say. But it is the same hollow 'yeah' that echoed in my TA's office three hours ago. Something doesn't feel right. The words ring from outside of me, trying to penetrate my paper-thin body, but they only manage to create a few light ripples across my shirt.

Khalid breaks my reverie, "I'm gonna do the 'roids if this doesn't work, man."

For a moment, I wonder if he means this. He sure sounds serious. I think of all those health classes where they warned us about the dangers of sports drugs. I remember TV images of hulk-like figures getting angry over the smallest things, then ripping fire hydrants out of their foundations. I see metal-detectors in high schools and people with tense, worried faces, flashing anger and lashing hatred. I see testosterone-driven men, throwing knives over lunch money and the latest video game cartridges.

"It's probably not a good idea," I say. "I mean, it's not worth it."

"How long you want to be like this, all lonely and no date?" Khalid says, "Are you just going to read books all your life? Fuck, man."

I realize that Khalid will not in any way be convinced otherwise, "Look," I say, "I need your help. I need something printed. It's an exam that I have to type for my TA."

"You get to type your exam? No shit."

"Not exactly. The TA didn't like my handwriting. It was so bad, it almost made her throw in the towel. I mean, if I don't get this printed and couriered back to her, I will be murdered."

Khalid laughs, "Yeah, your handwriting is worse than my kid sister's, and she's seven. Relax, brother. I've got you covered. Meet me at Weston Mall tonight. Close to the front entrance."

"What time?" I say.

"Eight o'clock," Khalid says. "Don't be late. And lend me some money while you're at it. This protein shit isn't cheap."

I decide I will have to compensate him for the printing. I take out thirty dollars from an ATM machine and head to the bus stop.

———

When I arrive at Weston Mall, I see Khalid. With a cigarette between his fingers, he stands close to the entrance, leaning against the hood of his dad's car. Dark shades cover his eyes, even though the sun fell some time ago. I involuntarily grin, and show all my crooked, stained teeth.

Khalid and I sit in the Volvo while I recount the sad experience with Ellen Sanders. I take the blue floppy disk from my dirty jacket pocket. I hand him the thirty dollars, all in crumpled bills.

Khalid fumbles the money into his shirt. "Thank you, Saah. Now let's get out of here and hit the clubs, man. I can hook you up with one of my friends' friends."

He glances over and looks me up and down, "On second thought, you should probably just sit in the corner, because you sure look like a bum." Khalid laughs between puffs of smoke.

"I'm not even thinking about this," I say.

"Well you should. You should, man." Khalid shakes his head. "You want to just spend all your life alone? Haven't you had enough of this life?"

"I guess," I say. But in my heart, I know I won't find what I need in a club.

But I can't say this to Khalid, any more than I could have said anything to Ellen Sanders. Why can't I?

Khalid scans me up and down with a fierce stare, "You don't care what anybody thinks of you, do you. You mean to tell me you'd rather read books than be with a girl?"

I shift in place.

Khalid gasps, "Are you nuts?"

I fumble for words, "Um, I don't know. It's not an either–or thing, is it?"

Khalid rolls his eyes, "This isn't the nineteenth century. It's 1994, for God's sake. Look, okay. You have your own style and everything. But your package, it stinks. Your pants are so skinny they look like pantyhose. Ugh. You need to eat. I am sure that someone will take you, but you'll wait a long time. You should lift weights, at least."

We spin around a few times like this, and then Khalid drops me at my parents' place. He promises to bring the printed version of my exam the following day. I thank him and wonder what will happen to the money I gave him. I think of money being pumped into protein supplements, drugs, or the latest self-improvement from one of those makeshift suburban offices. I cringe.

Student Welfare

Martha Sinclair

Wednesday July 13, 1977

The doorbell rings. By the time I get to the door of my first floor apartment on Fifth Avenue in Ottawa, I find Mom peeking out the window of her blue Datsun.

I cross the street and hunch toward her window.

"Why don't you come in for tea, Mom?"

"No."

Mom pushes a white business envelope through her window, "Don't open this. If you open this, I'll make sure you don't get welfare."

"Please, Mom. You've never been in my apartment. It'll just be you and me. Mark isn't home. I'll make you some Tetley tea."

Her Datsun putts away.

I stand in the street with the envelope. Mom hand-wrote "To Whom It May Concern" on it face.

The next morning, I stuff Mom's envelope into my beige, canvas army satchel. I secure its two frayed ties into their dented, rusty buckles for my bus ride up Bank Street to the downtown Ottawa welfare office.

I hurry out of the bus to make my 10:30 appointment. I ride a dark elevator to the third floor of the worn Social Services office block. I rehearse my answers to the questions my boyfriend's mother told me they'll ask.

"Don't let them know you live with Mark. If they find out you live with him, they won't give you student welfare. They'll expect him to support you," Mrs. Nelson said.

"I live with my roommate, Mark. We each have our own room. No, Mark's not my boyfriend," I practise again and again.

Normally, I use the front room of our apartment as an art studio, where I paint and draw in pen and ink on my brown melamine desk in the bay window. For the welfare inspection, Mark dragged my twin mattress into the room.

———

The receptionist tells me to take a seat and picks up the phone. I perch on a metal stacking chair in the tiled waiting room of the welfare office. She mutters into the black handset and eyes me.

I tuck my satchel tight into my lap. A large clock hangs behind the receptionist. The clock's spindly second hand flicks and taps around its face behind a yellow domed-glass cover.

A brown haired woman in her twenties calls my name and glances at me as I stand.

"Follow me," she says.

I trace her trail through cubicles constructed from brown fabric partitions. Her navy blue, lace-up shoes follow a worn path on the thin, grey carpet. Sharp creases fan out on the back of her navy-coloured linen dress.

She ducks into a glassed-in office in the far corner, points to a wooden chair and closes the door. I lower into the chair. She rotates a large, orange fabric chair, sits and scoots to her desk.

Stacks of white application forms and carbon-copied pages crowd her desk and behind her, faded posters and curled memos hang from thumbtacks on a sun-bleached corkboard.

"My name is Miss Stafford. I'm reviewing your application for student welfare." She adjusts her large metal-rimmed glasses and studies a typed form.

My satchel slips off my shoulder and thumps to the floor. I fumble with the strap and hoist it back onto my lap. I hold my breath.

"Where are you planning to go to school?" Miss Stafford asks.

"I enrolled for Grade 13 at Glebe Collegiate."

Miss Stafford flips through pages in a file, "According to your Grade 12 report card from Meadowvale High School you should have no problems getting in. Why aren't you living with your parents?"

"My mother kicked me out. She wanted me to be an accountant, but I told her I wanted to be an artist. She told me to move out by the end of the month if I didn't agree."

"Why accounting?"

"I got 90s in math. I offered to go to medical school instead of accounting. But Mom said 'no.'"

Miss Stafford studies me, scans my file, turns a page, and peers up. "In order to qualify for student welfare, your parents must state that they will not support you."

"My mother wrote a letter." I unbuckle my bag, pull out Mom's letter, and hand it to Miss Stafford. "I haven't opened it," I say.

Miss Stafford reads the envelope, "We'll have to confirm this letter with your mother."

"Mom said you could call."

Miss Stafford peels open the envelope and straightens out the folded sheet.

I clear my throat. Fluorescent lights sputter in the hallway.

Miss Stafford slides the letter into the file folder and shakes her head. My face burns. *What did Mom say?*

Miss Stafford asks me about my apartment on Fifth Avenue.

I stammer my rehearsed lines.

Miss Stafford peers from above the letter, "I'll need to do a home inspection if you qualify."

The beige venetian blinds above her open window shimmer in the July breeze.

"Will I be able to get student welfare?" I ask.

She closes my file, tosses it onto a pile and stands. "You will be sent a formal decision in the mail."

She leads me around the office dividers back to reception. I shuffle down two flights of stairs, step through the glass doors, wander down Rideau Street to the bus stop, and wait for the red and white OC Transpo bus. My feet sweat in my older sister's worn, brown leather shoes.

Frozen Beef

Martha Sinclair

November, 1977

My sister, Jeanie, and a tall, blond, teenaged guy squeeze through the narrow space between my boyfriend, Mark's, worn chesterfield and the four-foot-tall cupboard at the corner of our kitchen.

Jeanie drops her satchel on the cracked black and white tiled linoleum floor, pulls off her toque, and grins.

"Meet Glen." Jeanie tugs on Glen's beige canvas winter coat.

"Hi," Glen says, and his blue eyes search the floor. "Jeanie told me about you. I'm so glad to meet you."

"Really?" I say. "Take your coats off and I'll make tea."

"I wish I could, but I've got to be somewhere at three," Glen says.

"Glen's just dropped me off."

"I'll see you to the door," I say. I follow Glen back through the living room and open the frosted glass apartment door leading into the shared entrance of the three-storey, downtown Ottawa house.

"I'll stay longer next time. I mean, of course if you don't mind I come over again. With Jeanie, of course, when Jeanie comes over again." Glen's nose and cheeks redden. He stares at the stained and scratched hardwood floor.

"Sure, Glen," I tell him. "Come over again with Jeanie."

"That would be great." Glen shuffles into the entrance, pushes open the glass and wood outer door, nods, and bounds onto the porch and down the stairs.

I close our apartment door and tread back to the kitchen. Jeanie hunches, pulls out her high school text books and a black binder from her satchel, and drops them on the floor. She hoists out a green garbage bag, stands, and thumps it down on the grey laminate countertop.

"What's that?" I ask.

"It's for you." Jeanie peels the garbage bag back to reveal a frozen, raw, round roast of beef. "I took it from Mom's basement freezer."

I eye the cellophane-wrapped roast, "Don't you think Mom will notice it's missing?"

"Naw. That freezer is packed with stuff."

"Gee, thanks. Leave it out, and I'll cook it tonight."

"Good idea, it's started to thaw already. I brought it to school with me."

"What if she notices? You're not even allowed to talk to me."

"She won't," Jeanie says and slides her books back into her shoulder bag.

"Want tea?" I ask.

"Of course. I can stay for an hour or so, and then I've got to take the bus back home."

I pour water into our steel kettle, place it on the burner, and rotate the stove knob to "high."

Jeanie relaxes into the padded, vinyl kitchen chair and leans onto Mark's chipped, grey and white-swirled formica table.

I place two of Mark's square, Hawaiian, souvenir ceramic mugs on the table, spoon Twinings Earl Grey tea from its yellow tin into Mark's grey, Aladdin's lamp-styled tea pot, and drop into a chair at the table.

"So, who's Glen?" I ask Jeanie.

"My new boyfriend."

"He seems shy," I say.

"At first, but he's okay once he gets to know you."

"Bring him back anytime you want."

"Yeah. I will. He's got a car."

The kettle sputters and squeals. I stand, turn off the burner and pour boiling water into the teapot. I carry a green plastic jug with a sagging bag of milk from the fridge and arrange it with the teapot in the centre of the table.

"How's it going?" Jeanie asks.

"I'm working on my portfolio for my High School of Commerce interview."

"Have you applied yet?"

"No. They take applications in January. I'm trying to make more art for my portfolio. Wanna see my latest?"

Jeanie pours tea into the mugs, "Sure."

I wind through the narrow kitchen opening, into the living room, around my parents' worn, wooden coffee table, and into the front room. I clutch and carry a scrapbook-sized pen-and-ink drawing of Tangerine Dream's Peter Baumann back to the kitchen. "I've been working on this for a few weeks," I say.

Jeanie studies the drawing.

I point. "I'm still working on the details of his scarf."

"Wow, it looks real."

"Thanks. I really want to get into that special arts program."

I balance the drawing on a few fingertips, trudge back to my desk in the front room, and slide the drawing back under its protective sheet of tracing paper.

I drop back into my kitchen chair and sigh.

Jeanie says, "I'll bring more stuff from the freezer next time I come. I saw a chicken that's been in there forever."

"Just make sure you don't get caught. If Mom finds out you're talking to me or coming over here, she's going to get even stricter."

"Don't worry. I'll find a way to visit. She's not stopping me." Jeanie lifts her mug and slurps hot tea.

I pour milk into my mug of tea. Milk swirls and mixes with the dark amber liquid.

Miss Jones

Laura Raymond

I stand at the front of my classroom. I'm in the third week of a two-month, short-term teaching position at Primrose Primary School in London, England. My fourth-grade students sit at their clusters of desks, four to a group. They work on their art projects and whisper with their neighbours. Some students create pastel art using only blue, purple, and green, while others use only yellow, red, and orange. The students learn about the contrast between cool and warm colours.

I lean against my wooden desk, fold my arms across my chest, and survey the room. The students appear engaged in and focused on their work. I smile to myself.

Next door, Miss Jones erupts, "Sit down! No! Sit down right now!"

My students don't look up from their pastels.

"If you don't sit down right this instant, I'm sending you to the headmaster's office!" screams Miss Jones.

A few of my students peek at each other and snicker.

"That's enough," I tell them.

They get back to work. Some smile.

———

Miss Jones

My students work on their daily math challenge in small groups. I feel a buzz throughout the room as each group tries to complete the task first. I stroll around with my clipboard and take anecdotal notes on students' progress and collaboration.

Miss Jones storms into our classroom. She wears a white and black, horizontal-striped top with three-quarter length sleeves, tucked into a long, black skirt. Her dark, straight, smooth hair meets her shoulders, curled under in a bob. Her black leather boots make a distinctive click-clack sound as she walks.

I dare not ask who is watching her class in her absence.

"Do you have that math unit ready for me yet?" Miss Jones demands.

"I'm almost done," I say. "I was going to finish it today after school. I thought we weren't starting it until next week, though."

"Well I want to start it now," Miss Jones says. "Just make sure it's on my desk by tomorrow morning. I need it first period."

Miss Jones turns away from me before I can respond and click-clacks back to her classroom.

Later that afternoon, my students sit on the carpet, and I read them The Giving Tree by Shel Silverstein.

"GET OUT!" Miss Jones yells next door. "Get out right now! I've had enough of you!"

I pause. Some of my students turn toward the door. I focus my attention back on the book and read, "And the tree was happy . . . ."

Miss Jones's classroom door slams.

"Just a moment, boys and girls. Elisha, would you like to take over?" I say.

Elisha smiles, stands up, and sits in my rocking chair. She continues the story while I rush to the classroom door. I open the door and poke my head into the hallway. Miss Jones leans against the hallway wall with the tips of her fingers pressed against her forehead. She might be crying.

"Can I help you with anything, Miss Jones?" I ask.

Miss Jones peels her hands away from her face and slams her fists against her thighs. She stares at me, her blue eyes bloodshot and puffy, "You want to help me?"

"Well I, I mean if I can, yeah," I stammer.

"You want to know how you can help? Finish the math unit! That's how you can help!" Miss Jones pivots toward her classroom door, thrusts it open, stomps back into the room, and slams the door behind her. "Get back in your seats! Enough horseplay! Quiet! BE QUIET!"

I retreat back into my classroom, head last. My students stare at me from their seats on the carpet. Elisha holds The Giving Tree open, face down in her lap. I walk to the rocking chair and hold my hand out. Elisha stands up, gives me the book, and sits back down with her classmates.

I finish preparing the math unit after school. I stay late to make sure it's perfect. I print out two copies, one for me and one for Miss Jones. I leave a copy on her desk with a pink sticky note on top that says, "Let me know if you want me to change anything. Hope you have a good day!" I draw a smiley face at the bottom.

———

In mid-December, my short-term position ends. The regular teacher will be back from sick-leave in January. The staff throw me a goodbye party after school in the teachers' lounge. They serve cake, cookies, and samosas with tamarind sauce. Two-litre bottles of pop stand beside stacks of tiny, white styrofoam cups. We eat, we drink, and we tell funny stories about the students in our class-es. Miss Jones doesn't come to the party.

After cleaning up sticky paper plates and hugging colleagues goodbye, I trudge back to my soon-to-be former classroom to col-lect two reusable grocery bags filled with handmade cards and gifts that my students brought me.

I amble into the room and notice a small, blue envelope sitting in the middle of my empty desk. Tiny, tight handwriting loops my name on the front. I open the envelope. The card inside depicts blue, purple, and green irises on the front. Inside, a handwritten message reads, "I'll really miss you. Thank you for being so patient with me. Good luck, Lisa Jones."

I sit in my desk chair and reread the card several times. I fit the card back in its blue envelope and stuff it into one of the grocery bags. I take out a stack of yellow Post-It notes and write a short message to Miss Jones, "Thanks for the card, it was very appreci-ated and unexpected. I'll miss you too, and I hope we can stay in touch."

I pull the sticky note off its pad and let it linger on the tip of my middle finger. I examine the words I've written. I read them a few times, then I stand up, tuck in my desk chair, and sling both grocery bags over my shoulder. I take one last glance at my mes-sage to Miss Jones, still perched on my finger. I crumple the note into a ball and toss it in the waste-paper bin.

The Thin Blue Line

Loredana Polidoro

L isa and Bruna barrel up the walkway to the house, tossing knapsacks, jackets, and headbands on the grass.

"Loooredaaana!" The shrill sound of Lisa's singsong voice forces my neck muscles to tense.

I meet the girls at the front door, put on my fake smile, and proceed to fulfill my duties as an underpaid, overworked au pair in Paris.

"*Bonjour, les filles,*" I say.

Bruna capers into me and wraps her gangly arms around my hips.

Six months ago, I scoured the Internet for job prospects in Paris and found a website that matched nannies from around the world with families in Europe. Within minutes I created my profile, attached a recent picture, and dreamed of being the next Mary Poppins.

On my computer screen, the famille Chaise appeared to be exactly what I was looking for in a 'host family.' The mother was Italian, and the father was French. They were looking for an au pair to care for their two young daughters and brand new baby boy. They lived in an idyllic little town just outside of Paris called Montgeron. I searched the Internet for any information on what might become my new home. Pictures online revealed a tree-lined, sleepy suburb that housed one cinema, a tobacco store, and two boulangeries. My mother warned me, "If it looks too good to be true, it probably is." Eager to prove her wrong, I clicked the "Contact" button and forwarded my application to the Chaise family.

"Okay, *les filles. Subito laver before le goûter! Allez!*" I instruct the girls to wash up for their afternoon snack in a mixture of forgetful English, Grade 9 French, and my parents' Italian dialect.

The girls race off to the bathroom, giggling and singing at frequencies only dogs could understand. I gather their discarded outer-garments from the foyer, hang up their jackets and empty knapsacks, and start counting the hours until bedtime.

Lisa and Bruna sprint to the kitchen, crashing into me.

"*D'accord, les filles. Qu'est–ce que vous—*"

"Nutella!" Lisa and Bruna shout in unison.

I grab a long, thin baguette from the counter and spread the dark brown, shiny confection over the crusty bread.

Lisa and Bruna hover beside me and eye my knife-hand closely, scrutinizing my Nutella-to-bread ratio.

"*Je veux plus de Nutella,*" Bruna whines.

"*Moi aussi,*" Lisa wails.

I spackle another layer of hazelnut chocolate onto the baguette. The girls lick their lips. Lisa pushes her little sister aside, snatches the biggest piece, and runs to the TV room. Bruna exaggerates the force of the push, falls to the floor, and howls. I jump to slice another piece of baguette, spread the Nutella, and hand Bruna two pieces. She picks herself off the floor, clutches her snacks, and rushes to the other room to join her sister.

The *Bob L'éponge* theme blares from the television's speakers. Lisa and Bruna devour their snacks and laugh at the antics of Bob and his sea creature friends. I sit with the girls and try to follow along to the French-dubbed cartoon.

The blue digital clock on the DVD player catches my attention. My neck muscles tighten and my jaw flexes. I wonder how late the children's mother, Francesca, will be tonight.

Last night, Francesca came home hours after the girls went to bed. While she ate her dinner alone at the table, I asked her if she had purchased more Metro tickets for me to get into Paris this weekend—my only time off.

"I work all day to come home to you demanding things of me," Francesca spoke in impeccable English. Her parents passed her up-bringing on to foreign nannies, just as she does with her children.

"This place is a disaster. The girls are unhappy, and you think you deserve Metro tickets," Francesca snorted, and took a swig from her wine glass. She leaned back in her seat at the head of the table, clutching her glass.

I decided against asking about my paycheque, now two weeks overdue. "I'm sorry," I whispered and slumped out of the room. My feet moved quickly up the stairs and into my bedroom, down the hall from the master bedroom that Francesca shares with her husband, Michel. I threw my body onto my twin bed and cried into my Disney Princess pillow.

Tonight, Bruna wipes the chocolate from her face with the back of her hand. I spy Lisa sucking on her thumb, concealing her crime with her long hair. She catches me watching and swiftly pulls her hand from her face. She turns her back to me.

"Okay, *pas de TV*. Enough," I say and grab the remote control from the coffee table and shut the TV off.

"*Mais, non, Loredanaaaa,*" Lisa and Bruna mewl in high-pitched voices, igniting my now-chronic headache. They fight in Italian, but they whine in French.

"Let's colour at the kitchen table," I motion, colouring in the air with a marker.

Lisa and Bruna rush to splay their markers and colouring books on the table, fighting over colours. I pick the Tintin colouring book from the pile and begin shading in Snowy's black nose.

Baby Gabriel stirs from his nap and cries out. I climb up the marble staircase to the baby's room, right across the hall from my own. I pry open the door and spot Gabriel standing in his crib, gripping the rail. He smiles at me and reaches his arms out, anticipating a post-nap snuggle.

I pull Gabriel from the crib, squeeze him in my arms, and smell the top of his head. He coos and rubs his face on my chest. The girls argue over colours downstairs.

"Your sisters are nuts," I say to Gabriel in a baby voice.

The girls continue to fight, their Italian growing louder and angrier.

With Gabriel in my arms, I walk to the top of the staircase and yell down to the girls, "*Les filles, arête!*" Gabriel's body stiffens at the harsh rattle of my voice, and I feel the vibrations of his tiny heart speed up.

I take Gabriel back to his nursery, change his diaper, and dress him in his new Burberry onesie. "Shall we go downstairs and see your wacky sisters?" I coo.

Gabriel and I enter the kitchen, but the girls' seats are vacant. Down the hall, I spot Lisa and Bruna in the TV room, each sprawled on one of their step-father's pristine, white leather couches. Markers dangle from their fingers and litter the carpet.

"Lisa! Bruna!" I call.

Their bodies straighten and they turn to me, careful not to make eye contact.

My gaze lands on the wide, white armrest beneath Lisa's hand. A long, thin, blue line marks the leather. I gasp.

The door opens, and I hear heeled black dress shoes click on the marble floor. The sound creeps closer.

"*Allo, les filles. Ça va,* Loredana?"

"*Boujour,* Michel," my voice squeaks, barely audible.

Michel scoops Gabriel from my arms and bounces in place. He spots the blue line, and his eyes widen and his nostrils flare. My body freezes.

"*Qui a fait ça?*" Michel points to the line on the armrest.

"*Ce n'est pas moi!*" Lisa and Bruna both cry out.

Michel hands Gabriel back to me and walks toward Lisa. Tears pool in her eyes. A matching thin blue line adorns her left cheek.

Three weeks later, after another encounter with Francesca, I call my mom, back in Toronto.

"That woman is the devil, and those girls are her spawn. I can't take it anymore," I cry into the phone, sitting on the edge of my twin-bed.

"Well, Lore, you told them that you would stay until December, and it's only June," my mom's voice echoes through the long distance call.

"It's either, I come back home, or I jump off the Pont Neuf."

"Lore, come on. Don't joke about such things."

"The only reason I would stay is for Gabriel. And Michel."

I lower my voice and clutch the phone closer to my mouth, "I think he hates those girls more than I do."

Through the phone lines, I will my mother to decide what I should do and fix my predicament.

"It's up to you, Lore, if you want to stay or come home. I can't tell you what to do."

I sink deeper into the bed and wipe my nose with the back of my hand. "I'm coming home, mom."

She doesn't say it out loud, but, thousands of miles away, I sense my mother thinking, "I told you so."

Cigarette Money

Keith Brown

The Scarborough Rapid Transit train lurches along its narrow track toward McCowan station, the very last stop on the line. I peer outside at a row of houses that resemble flat, yellow and white boxes. The skyline fills with clouds, pink and hazy from an earlier rainstorm.

I clutch a piece of lined paper decorated with a map and scribbled handwriting. The RT doors open. I follow the crows out of the station and step out to the corner of McCowan and Bushby. Sweat clings to my clothes.

Concrete surrounds most of this part of Scarborough. Occasional crab-weeds and dandelions creep up from the sidewalk cracks. The air feels muggy, but comfortable. I let my mind wander as I pass commercial parks.

I wade through an industrial area with many indistinguishable warehouses. A few cars glimmer in the parking lots, and a few tired commuters recline against vinyl plastic seats.

The time on my digital watch reads "7:06 p.m." I snap out of my reverie. I am late for my first day of work.

The unmarked office hides at the back of an auto shop. I pull open a tinted glass door to reveal rows of desks under bright, fluorescent lights. Desks line up in single, narrow rows. I smell gasoline from the adjacent room. I hear the distant whine of a ratchet drill.

Pam greets me as I enter. She wears a brown dress, hoop earrings, lipstick, and heavy mascara. Blue eye shadow dapples the sides of her eyebrows and lashes. I sharpen my focus and notice sagging, blackened skin beneath her eyes.

"Great to finally meet you, and welcome to our happy family," Pam beams. Her arm fans toward the back of the room. A few employees linger over the coffee station. They wave and return to staring into their Styrofoam cups.

Pam crosses her arms. She appraises me up and down. My leather shoes feel damp and muddy from the puddles outside.

"And where are you coming from?" Pam asks.

"North York," I pause. "Sorry for my lateness."

"North York? Holy shit! I admire your dedication. You came all the way from North York to be here?"

"Well," I say. "This is actually my first job. I am not that familiar with the area."

Pam leads me to a cubbyhole in the back corner of the office, close to the auto shop. She motions for me to sit down. Papers, family photos, and two ashtrays litter her desk.

"Now, about the job . . . " Pam takes a deep breath and rests her chin on her hands.

"You know, as I said on the phone, we do intend to expand our operations in a few years. For the time being, this job is more like part time. Hope you don't mind. Nobody really lives off it. You can earn enough money for cigarettes and stuff."

Pam pauses. "Do you smoke?"

"Um, no."

"That's okay. It's not too late to start." Pam fidgets with a half-empty pack of Belvederes on her desktop.

I wring my hands, "This job, um, it's not just commission, right?"

"Well, um, yeah. That's another thing," Pam flecks stray ashes from her keyboard tray. "I told you, we sell a lot of kitchen stuff over the phone. And we donate a fraction to charity. Well, you know, not everyone cares about kitchen stuff. Or charity."

"I see," I say.

"So, in the beginning, we get you on the phone to see how well you can get the customers to buy our products. That's what, around here, we call the trial period."

Pam points to a sheet of chart paper taped to the wall behind her. Thick black marker traces a series of boxes. Colourful figures and arrows surround each box. A stick figure stands triumphant at the top of the paper and sports a dollar sign on his forehead.

"After your twentieth successful sale, we add base salary to whatever commission you make. We increase your salary after each increment of twenty sales. If you get over a hundred sales, you win a trip to Costa Rica. The company pays your ticket. Isn't that awesome?"

A motor revs from the adjacent room.

I cough. "Yeah . . . the thing is, I'm a student. I'm just hoping to get some work experience. And my family supports me a lot for my school. I guess money's secondary."

"I'm sure you'll be fine," Pam says. "And, you know, we're like family. We support each other." Pam winks.

A man with a muscle shirt and thin moustache strides into the room. He plops a Tim Horton's coffee and a bag of cookies on Pam's desk.

"Thank you, sir," Pam says.

"My pleasure, madam."

The two exchange glances and start to laugh. They confer in muted voices for several minutes.

Red heat flushes my cheeks. I clear my throat. The man turns around, spots me, and thrusts out an oil-stained hand.

"Oh, sorry, Keith, this is Rex," Pam says. "He's from the auto-shop next door. Rex and I share the rent on this unit."

Rex grins and raises his eyebrows. His lips part into a rounded "O" shape, "New blood?" he mutters.

Pam laughs and slaps Rex on the back, "C'mon, Rex, don't scare him! It's his first day."

Rex guffaws and bounces out of the room.

Pam motions me to the main room. She shows me a desk with a unit number on its side, a headset, and half a piece of paper, containing the script.

"This will be your workstation," Pam announces. She finds a stray chair in one of the aisles and kicks it toward the desk. "You are desk number seven."

Pam shows me a page full of phone numbers with last names beside them. She says, "Maybe I can get you to start on a few of the easier numbers. These are the first-timers. These folks have never been contacted before. Once you get used to these, we'll give you the tough nuts. Those second-timers can get nasty."

I stare at the sheet of numbers. It looks like a photocopied excerpt from the white pages. A few names appear blurred, and ink stains blot out the numbers at the bottom of the sheet.

"Do you want me to finish this row in one night?" I ask.

"Well, do what you can. I'm going easy on you, since it's your first day. Over time, you'll be able to sail through the list. No problem." Pam gives me a "My Name is" sticker tag, printed in blue letters.

I scribble my name onto the tag and pin it next to my heart. Pam leads me through a row of tired faces.

"Everyone, this is our new addition to the family. Please say hello to Keith. Feel free to buy him a coffee," Pam snorts.

A few faces break into strained grins. Some snicker. Soon, they resume their hunched positions over their phone lists.

A young girl in her early-twenties sits behind me and gives me a passing nod. She adjusts her round glasses and glides her finger down the sheet in front of her, close to the bottom. I gaze down at her list of numbers. Red marks fill the page, with several product names and dollar signs beside each.

Pam leans into me and whispers, "That's Sally. She's been here only a few weeks. She's the rising star of the team. She's a university major, just like you. English, or sociology, or something like that. See, there's light at the end of the tunnel. You just have to be patient and believe in the cause."

I sink down in my chair and listen to Sally's voice. She talks in fast, chirpy tones. The voice on the other end grates against her headset. Sally remains unfazed. She drops the call and nimbly dials the next number.

I glance down at the script and take a deep breath. I pencil my own name in the blank space on the script.

I dial my first number: Sharp, M.

"Who is this?" A man's voice emerges from a sea of static.

"Um, my name is Keith? And I'm from a charity organization called Coping in Tough Times. Do you have a minute? I want to tell you about some exciting products, all for a good cause."

"Yeah, well, I already got a call from you guys earlier. I told you not to call me again."

The phone list in front of me reads "First Timer" on its header. I raise my eyebrows. My jaw clenches.

"Sorry about that, sir. Was it perhaps another charity? I mean—"

The man's voice fizzles into a dry monotone, "No, I know. You're the guys who sell garbage bags, paper plates, shit like that, right? Not interested. What kind of charity sells garbage bags? You guys are crooks. Don't call me again."

The voice cuts out. A dial tone kicks in.

I cross out the first name on my list.

I remember Pam telling me that this is the trial period. I think of a story I read in grade school, "The Twelve Trials of Hercules." I arch my shoulders and suck in my chest.

Number Two. Abdelhaleem, A. I skim through the script again. I tap the numbers on the phone's keypad.

Someone picks up after the third ring. I hear traffic sounds and a radio in the background.

"Hello, is Mr. or Mrs. Abdelhaleem there?" I try in my gentlest voice. It makes a raspy echo on the other end.

"This is he," a man's voice says.

I twist the crumpled script in my hand.

"Look, sorry to bother you. I am just, um . . . I am calling on behalf of a charity organization called Coping in Tough Times. We sell various items at wholesale prices. Proceeds go to a charity that helps subsidize low-income residents."

Heavy breathing presses against the mouthpiece. Traffic sounds intensify.

The man's voice resurfaces, "Coping in Tough Times, huh? You want to give me some of that money? I am coping in tough times, too."

My eyes dart through the script again. Blood tingles through my face and scalp. I can't find anything that says how to help people apply for the charity.

I scramble for words, "Um, yeah. Well, yeah, I know."

"You know what? What do you know? Look around you. I have six mouths to feed and two cars. Wake up, it's the recession. What a joke, coping in tough times. Aren't we all?"

"Okay, sorry to bother you. But thanks for your time."

The voice on the other end clicks out. The traffic and music come to a halt. The still and stuffy room re-emerges around me.

My third phone number takes me to a voice mail. Relief floods my forehead. I read off the script after the long beep. I improvise, "Sorry to bother you," then add in, "Hope you're having a great evening," at the end of the message.

By the fourth number, I get a "maybe." Mrs. Abigail says she'll speak to her husband and get back to me. I leave her the company's number and my personal extension. I pull out a red marker and scrawl "Maybe" beside her name and number. I smile. Four out of forty numbers have red marks through them. Thirty-six more to go.

Pam stops us for a coffee break and, what she calls, a "group huddle." We roll our chairs into the common area and form a haphazard circle. Some lean back in their chairs, others massage their half-closed eyes.

Pam displays a series of bar graphs with desk numbers beside them.

"Now look–it," Pam points a finger at the coloured bars. She traces an imaginary line through the slopes of March and then spirals her hand down the April slump.

"Sales are at an all-time low right now. I don't know why, but maybe because of tax season. Don't be surprised if you get a lot of "no's" tonight. But I want some positive vibes from you guys, okay? Don't give up. Let's see some momentum."

Pam claps her hands and lists off the top sales for the week.

Desk Number Six is the top earner.

I recognize the desk number as Sally's.

A faint smile cracks through Sally's puckered lips. She dashes to the centre of the circle to pick up a hand-signed certificate from Pam. Everyone else slouches deeper in their chairs. They twiddle their thumbs and fix their eyes on the bare floor.

Pam tears the coloured graph down to reveal a series of dollar figures and happy faces.

"This quarter, we are offering first, second and third prizes for the top sellers. A trip to Costa Rica, a year's subscription to *Time* magazine, and a refurbished car, donated by Rex's Auto! Whoo–hoo."

A few claps break out. The huddled bodies wave their arms and confer with each other. They compare notes on which prize they prefer.

They disperse with the shuffle of tired feet.

We wheel ourselves back to our desks. Sally's phone blinks red. My phone remains dark in the corner.

Sally goes straight to fielding calls. I try a few more numbers on my list and hope to reach the bottom by shift's end. Many of the contacts don't understand English, or somehow cannot hear me. I practice using a loud, bold voice. My volume encourages the other callers around me to raise their volume as well. Soon, I compete with a dozen other booming voices.

Pam stands at the doorway of her cubbyhole, grinning.

I fly through fifteen contacts and leave messages for half of them. I keep my hopes up for a return call.

I pack up to leave the office at nine sharp. Some of the others also pack up. A few stragglers stay behind to make more calls. Sally proceeds through her second list.

I turn around before exiting the office. Pam and Rex have returned to flirting. I see a sign-up sheet for people to come in, beside the table of daily sales quotes and rankings.

Nobody looks up as I leave.

I return to McCowan Station by half past nine. I peer through the train windows. The dark sky hides the rows of houses. Instead, I see my own reflection, distorted in the glass. I pick up a book and read for the remainder of the trip.

The RT yawns back into Kennedy Subway Station. I begin the long journey over and up to Sheppard Station. I take my red and black address book out of my bag and scan for other potential jobs. Sales jobs flood the page. Telesales, to be specific. Commission and semi-commission sales. Few of them are full time. None of them promise a weekly salary.

I take a blank page and sketch a graph of my day's progress. Fifteen out of forty contacts, makes thirty seven percent. Less than half of my target. And, of those fifteen, most were messages on answering machines. Three of them might return my call.

I estimate that it will take me at least three months to reach halfway to Sally's sales. And all for cigarette money.

I arrive home at ten thirty. I crawl into bed and fall asleep soon after my head hits the pillow.

I never go back to that office.

Bowties and Telenovelas

Sandra Campoverde

"Mija?" Papi says.

I close the door, I put down my backpack, and wipe the sweat off my forehead. "Yeah, Papi."

I unbuckle my sandals and place them next to his orthopaedic shoes. I pull my hair up in a ponytail. A small light glows from the living room.

"Did I miss it?" I ask.

"No, no. The Univision news is still on," Papi says.

At six o'clock every evening, Papi and I start our marathon of Hispanic telenovelas. Tonight's schedule includes Más que Sabe el Diablo, Eva Luna, and Esmeralda. For three consecutive hours we fixate on storylines based on crying, screaming, cheating, drama, tricksters, and drug cartels.

"Hola, Papi." I bend down and kiss both of his cheeks. First the left one, then the right. "How was your day?" I ask.

"Oh, you know. Tiring. Cleaning, cooking, peeling potatoes—"

He smiles and attempts to lift himself from the couch using the armrest for support. He grunts.

"Papi, just stay there."

"No, no, I can do it," Papi waves his hand in a stopping motion. He attempts once more to rise from his seat. His face turns red. He inhales, sits up, and exhales.

I scurry toward the loveseat. I pick up the grey, custom-made pillow that was designed specifically for his back three years ago. His physiotherapist, Dr. Rahiem, says it will help with back support.

"Sandra, I made your favourite sopita," Papi says.

I prop the pillow behind his back. "Bow-tie?" I say.

Papi nods and smiles, "Yeah, I'll serve you a bowl. It's still hot."

My dad prides himself on his soup made with potatoes and bow-tie pasta. It reminds him of Ecuador. It reminds him of the countryside. It reminds him of how poor they were.

"Papi, it's okay. You sit. I can serve myself."

I walk towards the kitchen and hear grunts. I turn around, "Dad, what are you doing? Stay on the couch."

"Sandra, come on. I'm not dead, you know."

I inch towards him.

"No. Stop," he says.

I stop and watch him. He grunts, inhales, exhales, and lifts himself off the couch. Sweats drips from his forehead. Papi glances up at me, grins, and limps past me toward the kitchen.

Papi waves me over and says, "Sit down."

I adjust myself on one of the cognac-stained chairs Mami ordered two months ago. Papi opens the dish cupboard and pulls out a white bowl, imprinted with faded flowers.

Papi glances at my engagement ring, "This is the last time I'm serving you as a Campoverde. Tomorrow you'll be a Centofante."

He serves two scoops of soup into the bowl. "You know, Sandrita. You're gonna be on your own now."

Papi struggles toward the round, cognac-stained table, sets down my bowl of soup, and plops down on the chair across from me, "When I told my mom I was leaving for Canada, she begged me to stay. She cried. She pleaded. I told her I needed to make my own life."

My papi grew up without a father. He provided income for himself, his mother, and his younger brother. He put food on the table for all of them.

"Sandrita, when you have kids, you're going to learn so many things," he says.

I plunge the worn, silver-tinted spoon into my bowl, "Oh? Like what?"

I tilt my head above my soup bowl and carry the spoon to my mouth. The steam from the broth fogs up my glasses. I blow.

"You're going to learn that one day your kids are gonna leave you and make a life of their own," Papi says.

I slurp the broth.

He smiles, "Good?"

"Mmhmmmmmm."

"Good," Papi smiles.

"Papi, you know I'm gonna come visit you," I say.

"I know."

"I'm gonna live a five-minute walking distance."

"I know."

"Like, I'm gonna see you all the time. All the time."

Papi laughs.

"I'm gonna miss you so much," I say.

"I know," he blows me a kiss. I pretend to catch the kiss and giggle.

"Papi, you remember!"

He says, "Of course I remember. How can I forget something like that?"

I smile, bite my lip, gulp, and squint. I gaze down at my bowl.

When I was seven years old, I watched Full House on repeat. I always wanted Papi to tuck me into bed. On Full House, the dad, Danny, always tucked the children in. One night, after playing Barbies with Papi, I asked him to tuck me into bed. I remember he didn't say anything at first, but then he smiled when I took his hand and tugged him off the couch. We held hands and walked up the lilac-carpeted staircase to my room. I rushed to my bed, jumped up, kicked off my Bugs Bunny duvet, and positioned myself under my sheets. He stared, smiled, and stood by the staircase. I waved him over and watched him follow my instructions for "tucking in." He took the sheets and the duvet, and he placed them over me. He made sure my arms were over the duvet. He fluffed my pillow and kissed me on the forehead. Before he left my bedroom, I called his name. He looked over and I blew him a kiss. He laughed and asked what he had to do next. I told him to catch it. Every night and day after that, he caught all of my kisses and sent me many, too. We stopped ten years ago.

"Sandrita?" Papi says.

I look up at him and whimper. Papi pushes himself up from his seat, walks toward me, bends over, and embraces me. "Don't worry. I'll still make you bow-tie soup."

"And how about the telenovelas?" I say.

I hear the opening credits to Más que Sabe el Diablo on TeleLatino.

I sob. Papi kisses my wet cheek, strokes my hair, and holds me close.

Ten Dollar Taxi

Ken Levine

8:20 p.m.

I swing on my jacket. I feel both pockets for my wallet, phone, and earbuds. I slam the front door shut and bolt down the stairs. Please, let the subway be on time.

Spotlights bounce off Casa Loma, on top of the hill. I scurry to the southbound subway platform at Dupont Station. The screen above me reads, "Next Train 2 min." I exhale.

I met Jenny last Friday, Valentine's Day, at a rave in a five-storey, abandoned building, west of Dufferin Grove. We talked about teachers' college, danced to beats spun by Tricky Moreira under hand-cut paper hearts, drank cans of Pabst Blue Ribbon, and I asked for her number.

8:40 p.m.

I dash off the streetcar, at the corner of Dundas and Ossington, with just enough time to grab cash from TD Bank. I slow my pace to keep from sweating and stride down Ossington Avenue. I pass The Communist's Daughter, The Painted Lady, and Hawker Bar with its neon red sign, PROVE THAT YOU LOVE ME AND BUY THE NEXT ROUND. I need to get to the bar before she does.

What does she look like again? I fixate on Bellwoods Brewery's red, bell-shaped sign.

8:55 p.m.

I stop, take a deep breath, and ease into Bellwoods. Metal, industrial-style light fixtures hang overhead. The table chatter and music echoes off the loft-high, concrete walls. A chalk board runs the length of the northern wall and lists bottled beers from Abbey Grand Cru to Zywiec Pilsner.

I scan for the hostess and rehearse, "you look nice," hug Jenny, "you look nice," hug Jenny.

A woman in a grey knit hat, blue scarf, and black leggings leans against the wall.

She steps toward me, "Hi."

"Oh, hi," I answer. No hug. No, "you look nice."

Jenny stands taller and looks bigger and older than I remember.

"I didn't expect you to get here before me," I say.

"I live close by."

"Did you talk to the hostess?" I ask.

"Yes, a table should be ready soon."

The hostess waves us over and we follow.

I perch on a bar stool at a raised, round table for two. A glass partition separates us from tall vats of brewing beer. I peek over Jenny's shoulder. An iPad displays album art for the current song, "Beach Comber" by Real Estate.

The server fills two glasses with water. "Can I get you something to drink?"

Jenny orders a draft. Stay Classy. 2.8% alcohol. Seven dollars.

I order a draft. Bring Out Your Dead. 10% alcohol. Seven dollars.

"Oh, and can you leave the water here?" Jenny asks.

"Sure." The server sets the pitcher of water beside her.

Jenny reads the menu, "Those duck hearts look interesting."

"You should try them. My roommate likes them. I can't have any, though, since I'm a pescaterian."

"Oh . . . what is that again?"

"I've been a vegetarian for about ten years, but now I also eat fish."

The server places down our drinks, "Can I get you anything to eat?"

Jenny orders the duck hearts. Seven dollars.

I order the fries. Five dollars.

Jenny takes a sip of beer. I raise mine towards her, "Cheers."

"Oh." She pulls the glass from her lips and clinks. "Cheers."

I lean forward, "So, what do you do?"

She fills her cup with water and takes a swig of beer, "I work at an organization for gay rights."

Or, maybe it was an organization where a lot of gay people worked. My eyes wander from the vats of brewing beer, to the servers, to the the signboard. Jenny doesn't watch TV. I wonder how many kinds of beer they make at once? Jenny doesn't listen to much music. I should listen to that Real Estate album again. Jenny doesn't read.

"So what exactly do you every day after work?" I say.

Jenny takes a gulp of water, "Monday, I go to the gym. Tuesday, I volunteer as a Big Sister . . . "

Before she gets to Wednesday, I begin a tangent about working with kids, and how that must be so rewarding and a big commitment on her part, and how I volunteered at an elementary school by my place, and that I wish I was still doing it.

9:20 p.m.

She pinches a duck heart and pops it into her mouth.

I grab some fries, "How are they?"

"What?"

"The duck hearts, do you like them?"

She pushes the plate off to the side, "They're okay. Kind of tough. Nothing special, really."

I smirk, "So, I'm not missing much, eh?"

The server reaches for the pitcher of water and fills Jenny's glass, "Can I get you another round?"

Jenny orders a beer from the chalk board. A Fruli, strawberry beer. 4.1% alcohol. Six dollars.

I order a draft, Farmhouse Classic. 7% alcohol. Seven dollars.

"It's funny," Jenny continues, "I don't know why I even went to that rave. I guess since a few of my friends were going, I thought it might be fun. It was definitely interesting. I don't usually stay up so late anymore . . . "

The music drowns out her voice. I glance at the album art on the iPad. My eyes widen and I slam my pint glass on the table, "I know this song!"

"Uh, what?"

"I can't remember the name, but I recognize it," I say.

"Oh?"

I point behind her to the iPad, "What is it, what is it? I can usually tell based on album art."

"Oh . . . " Jenny finishes her beer and washes it down with the rest of her water. " . . . well, as I was saying, I usually go to this bar, Clinton's. It's right by my place. Do you know it? It has a patio, so it's great during the summer . . . "

I nod at Jenny, and I attempt to decipher the album art.

" . . . and I can't wait for Spring. It's my favourite seas—"

"It's Grizzly Bear!" I gasp, "How did I not remember that right away? I saw them live in Amsterdam for my roommate's birthday, and we had to get tickets there last minute, and we didn't think we would get tickets, but this couple had extras and sold them to us for face value, and then we saw them here at Roy Thomson Hall and we had such amazing—Oh, sorry, you were saying?"

She empties the vase of water into her glass and drinks, "I don't remember. I need to use the ladies' room. Sorry, I drink a lot of water when I drink."

"Oh. No worries. I didn't even notice."

She eases off the stool and saunters past me. I pull out my phone and swipe the password. I scour the bar. A man gathers glasses filmed with leftover beer. I squint at the iPad. It shows a picture of the artist Annie Clark's pale white face and curly, short brown hair on an orange background. "Actor" by St. Vincent plays.

10:50 p.m.

The server swoops in with a full pitcher of water, "Another round?"

"Oh, thanks. I was just about to ask for some more water."

Jenny orders a draft. Cat Lady. 7.2% alcohol. Seven dollars.

I order a draft. 3 Minutes to Midnight. 10% alcohol. Seven dollars.

I tap on the menu, "Do you like olives?"

"Yes."

"And an order of olives, please."

Five dollars.

After three beers, one glass of water, and fries, I excuse myself to the washroom.

This girl can talk, and I can't hear her above the music and noise of the bar, and this girl looks older and different than at the rave, and she isn't even into house music, and this bill will be expensive, and how much water and beer can she drink? And I better hurry so she doesn't think I'm taking a shit.

She checks her watch, "It's getting kind of late."

"It's only midnight."

She chugs the remainder of her beer and water, "All this beer made me tired."

"Okay," I raise my index finger as the server passes by, "just the bill, please."

"And–some–more–water," Jenny chirps.

———

We sway up Ossington towards Dundas. People stream in between and around us. I hail a cab. The taxi radio hums, a streetcar screeches. As the taxi approaches Jenny's street, she fiddles with her purse and sneaks out a bill. My head spins, and the haze of my beer buzz keeps me silent. She gazes out the window with her body pinned against the cab door. She clutches the cash in her hand.

"It's coming up," she says. "Pull over here."

She slides the bill into my hand, "Goodnight."

"Night. I'll—"

Jenny slips out of the cab, slams the door shut, and scampers up a stone path to her house apartment. I stuff Jenny's ten-dollar bill into my pocket and tell the cab driver "Dupont and Spadina." And I just spent over eighty dollars on drinks, food, and the rest of the taxi, and I know I will never see her again.

Leaving

Stefanie Turner

I suffocate in John's cramped bedroom on the second floor of his duplex in Outremont, Montreal. I stretch out my left arm and run my fingertips over the beige plaster wall, full of minuscule cracks that I have spent months learning. I commit a new portion of the wall to memory each visit. A stream of sun sneaks through the window. John hung navy blue, flannel sheets up when he moved into the apartment eight months ago, as a temporary solution to block the morning sun. The flannel sheets were pulled half way back last night, so a July breeze creeps in, along with the first light of day.

The familiar instinct to escape washes over me, followed by a wave of guilt that starts in my stomach and spreads through me. I ease myself over on the double mattress, my arm inches from John's side. He sleeps.

Last night we celebrated John's mother's seventieth birthday. We drove from my apartment in Toronto. I did not want to leave. John pleaded. I packed two suitcases full of clothes, enough to last me the rest of the summer.

"That was the plan," John said. "You are moving to Montreal for the summer—a trial, for when you move here permanently."

I've always been good at following plans, at doing what I'm told. So I threw the contents of my dresser drawers into the bag. "Do this quickly," I told myself.

By 11:00 a.m., we carried my suitcase into the parking lot of my condo on Spadina Avenue. John organized the trunk of his hatchback Mazda 3. My legs shook in the front passenger seat. I jolted when his hand grabbed mine.

"Ready, babe?"

"No," I thought.

"Yep," I nodded.

Once we passed Belleville, we fell into the routine of the drive along the 401. We had grown accustomed to it over the two and a half years of our long distance relationship. I skimmed through the songs listed on his iPod, past U2, past Eric Lapointe, past Coldplay, and stopped on Lifehouse. John drove. We stopped at Wendy's in Cornwall for spicy chicken burgers and fries.

We picked up John's parents at their home, a fifteen-minute drive from John's apartment. His parents spoke English to me and French to John during the ride into the city. His mother wore a blue sundress and the necklace we brought her from Venice last summer. When we arrived at the Argentinian restaurant in the Plateau for John's mother's party, she asked me to sit beside her. She introduced me to her friends, and I smiled and shook their hands. They told me I had a beautiful smile, asked if I spoke French or Spanish, inquired as to when I was moving to Montreal, and admired the way John and I looked as a couple.

I slide out of bed and tiptoe to the bedroom door. The wood floor creaks and moans under my feet. I unplug my cell phone from the charger in the wall and grab it off the floor. I inch the door closed behind me. The apartment is silent, except for the slow drip of the air conditioner in the front window. I pace the hallway that separates the kitchen and living room. Photos I took with the camera John bought me for Christmas two years ago cover the wall. I framed the frozen images of London's red telephone booths, Dublin's pub-littered streets, and Costa Rica's tangled-vine jungles for John's thirtieth birthday. I gaze past the pictures of our trips and focus on my own blurred reflection in the frames' glass. I tread to the end of the hallway and unlatch the linen closet door. John cleared the closet for my things. I snatch a pair of torn jeans and a black tank top, pull the clothing on, and slide my feet into the flip-flops lying on the black welcome mat. My hand touches the steel front door knob as the bedroom door creaks open.

"Are you leaving?" John's voice aches with hurt.

Yes, I think to myself. I say, "I'm just going for a walk by the water. I should be back soon."

"Is everything okay?" John asks.

I nod. The door closes.

I wipe my feet on the welcome mat. I hear the shower running. I pace into the living room and notice my suitcase now sits at the foot of the couch. It lies there, unzipped, top open, ready to be filled. The shower stops. John emerges from the bathroom with tousled hair, a bare chest, and reddened eyes.

He takes a slow breath in, "I checked the train schedule. The first departure to Toronto leaves in two hours. That should be enough time to pack up . . . if that's what you want." He slides past me into his bedroom and shuts the door behind him. I swallow the doubt at the base of my throat, walk to the linen closet, cradle a heap of clothing in my arms, and drop it into the suitcase.

Left Behind

Keith Brown

Kat's apartment sits in a thirty-storey high-rise, facing St. Michael's Hospital. Helicopters hum through the blinds.

I never get to see where the helicopters carry their passengers. I never learn what happens to them. But I hear them every time I visit Kat.

Kat stands on her queen-size bed and peels pictures off her wall. One is a photocopy of a kitten dangling from a tightrope, about to fall. The words *Oh Shit* appear handwritten in the background. Kat yanks the picture down. Thumbtacks tinkle through the crack between the wall and the bed.

Kat's bare feet slide across piles of magazines, clothes, and books. She struggles to balance herself by pinning her hands against the wall. She searches on the shelves above her bed for the missing sets of lipstick that her mom ordered for her through a catalogue. Soon she yields and pretends to fall, weak. She leans into my shoulder and presses her cheek against mine.

"You'd better help me pack this shit after I leave," Kat mumbles. She wraps her right arm around my neck for support, "I'm not gonna be able to carry this myself."

Kat just graduated from university. She studied zoology. Before that, she attended a prestigious boarding school in Toronto.

Kat grew up in a small town in Northern China. Now that she's finished her Canadian schooling, her parents want her to come back to China. They call her every evening to demand that she gets a high paying job, preferably close to Qianjin district, where she grew up. They even have a house picked out for her, close to where they live.

Kat scopes out a conservation job in Beijing. Conservation is her university major, but she doesn't savour city life.

Kat's dad has a business that sells bras and underwear. Kat's mom is in the newspaper industry. She dishes out information on what to eat, what to drink, and how to live. She claims that New Zealand is the world's safest place because it has the most organic milk in the world.

Kat hands me the keys to her rented flat. She sinks onto her bed and slides closer to me. She identifies each key with her fingers.

"Here's the outside key, and here's the inside. And this one is for the mailbox. Help me find my lipsticks when I leave. It's the Lancôme set I want, the one with the gold caps. That shit's so expensive. I can't afford to leave it behind."

Kat adjusts her thick glasses and tucks her bottom lip into her front teeth. She gazes back at the floor.

Ziplock bags of assorted makeup lie at her feet. Kat examines them, one by one. She stuffs them into various compartments of her pink and black luggage. Her luggage becomes lopsided and various pointed shapes jut out from its sides, as though hidden weapons wait to strike.

I offer to help with the packing, but Kat insists on inspecting each item first to see if it's worth taking. Most of it stays in colourful piles on the floor, destined for recycling.

"There's no way that we can pack all of this by the end of the afternoon. What are we going to do with the rest of it?" I ask.

Kat shrugs. She applies apple balm to her cracking lips.

"Just leave it here. Let the landlord deal with it. I lived here too long. No wonder I have too much stuff."

"Your landlord will take care of it? He's going to need a shovel to move all this." I wonder if I am partly to blame. After all, I suggested taking Kat to the zoo the previous weekend, and there was the trip to Centre Island the week before. Then, there were the past couple of days, when Kat asked me to do nothing with her all day. We spent quality time, just doing nothing.

I feel guilty. Should I have reminded her to start putting things away?

All month, we avoided the topic of luggage. We dreaded the inevitable day when Kat would have to pack. Doing nothing with Kat felt both irresponsible and delightful.

Kat's father and friends kept asking her, "Have you finished packing yet?"

"Not yet," Kat would say. "Give it a couple of days."

It has only been two months since I met Kat. We met in June, 2012. It is August first now, and Kat's school visa just expired.

"I wish you could stay," my voice falters.

"I know. But there's no way I can find work here in this short a time. Besides, my dad had a fit when I suggested working in Toronto."

"How about your mom? You and your mom should be able to talk him into it."

Kat frowns, "Mom wants me to marry a quality guy and settle in China."

"Quality guy? Oh yeah, right. She sounds like she is talking about New Zealand milk."

Kat laughs, "You know what I mean. Anyway, we talked about this before. She says you're too old for me. And not good looking enough."

Kat grins as she runs her fingers through my hair.

"You know, whatever happens, I hope we stay in touch," I murmur. "I'll visit you for sure."

"Yeah," Kat sighs. She gets up from her perch on the bed. "But give me a couple of months to settle."

"Yeah, sure," I agree. I have no idea what will happen.

I shuffle over to her mini-kitchen. A half-empty can of Sapporo sits on the counter. Yesterday, one of Kat's friends, Thomas, came over to help her pack.

Kat sees me eyeing the Sapporo. "Thomas was exhausted from yesterday's packing. I let him sleep over. He was barely moving."

"Oh, yeah," I say. I try to imagine brawny, grinning Thomas in his lumberjack shirt. I push away the thought of him, flopped out on Kat's comforter. I imagine him taking up most of the bed and can't imagine where Kat would have slept.

Kat pads into her bathroom to take a shower.

I look back at the warm can of Sapporo. I wonder what will happen to all the things Kat leaves behind. What will she miss? How does she know what to take with her and what to leave behind?

After Kat showers, we change into clean clothes and sprint into the streets. We plan to donate some of Kat's books and magazines.

Dundas Square bustles with live music. I lug a large plastic bag in my right arm, filled with *National Geographics*. Kat walks close beside me. She wears a light green dress and navy blue sandals.

We have enough time to go to Panera, where we order our favourite breakfast, chai latte with a bear claw. We climb the stairs to the second floor dining area after getting our lattes. The sun feels menacing and intrusive and lights up flecks of dust which dance around our shiny mugs.

"I figure if you can get a job at Toronto Greenpeace, you've got it made." My mouth spouts optimism. The latte gives me a brief burst of energy and anything seems possible.

"Maybe in two years. I dunno. Like I said, it's all up in the air." Kat grimaces. "Maybe my parents might warm up to the idea later. But, you know, they already bought a house for me and everything. Kinda sucks."

"Doesn't make sense why you studied here for half your life and then have to leave." I chew on the last crumbs of pastry before slugging back cold latte. "Besides, aren't there more conservation jobs in Canada?"

"Nah, China is really into protecting the environment. They have lots of smog from industry. Especially in Beijing."

Kat gazes into the cityscape outside the window. She sighs, "Sure I'll miss it. But, sometimes you just have to go where you need to go. It's like you go through something, suffer, then get through it. It's no big deal."

"You make leaving Toronto sound like a minor surgery."

Kat laughs. "Yeah, I do."

Kat and I leave Panera. The sky becomes overcast as we amble over to the used book store. We approach the buy–and–sell counter and I expect the store clerk to accept our fifty magazines. I wonder who hasn't savoured *National Geographic* as a young child.

The store clerk takes one quick glance into the stack of yellow spines. He shakes his head and rubs his hands into cheeks of grey stubble.

"Look, man, nobody buys *National Geographic* in stores any-more. Nobody." The clerk smells of cigarettes and unwashed dogs. He hunches into his stacks of books.

"Really?" I say. "I'm surprised. Do you know of anywhere that would take them?" I am in no mood to bargain. Time is running out.

"Damn things are less than twenty bucks for a year's subscription. I would suggest you just throw 'em out. Nobody will take 'em. But not on my premises. I've got enough books to take care of," he says and shoos the magazines away with his meaty palms.

Kat and I lurch out of the bookstore, dejected. I cringe at the thought of lugging the magazines back to Kat's apartment.

"Maybe I should take them home," I say. "I used to love those books when I was young."

Kat nudges my arm, "Forget it. He's right. Who buys National Geographics in a store, when you can get them online?"

She motions me over to the white bin of ninety-nine cent bargain books. She points to a spot where we can leave the magazines.

"You're not thinking of putting them there?" I gasp.

"Come on!" Kat says. "Anyway, nobody will notice."

"That guy was so pissed. He said he didn't want any of those things near his property. He'll think we're dumping on his premises."

I stand in front of Kat, trying to block the clerk's view.

"You worry too much, Keithie." Kat bends down and places the books on the rack, close to an Alfred Hitchcock anthology.

Kat retrieves the top issue in the stack before abandoning the pile.

"But you can keep this one. It's interesting."

I look at the issue Kat salvaged from the pile. It reads, "Polygamy in America," and there's a grinning cowboy on the cover. I pause. Reluctant, I stuff the magazine into my knapsack.

My mind goes back to the week when we first met. Kat told me about her past loves and how it was impossible for her to stay with only one person. She told me her heart was too large and too wide for one person.

The sky appears foreboding now. Rain splotches our unprotected clothes as Kat and I return to her apartment to do some last-minute packing. Soon, Janusz will arrive to pick us up and take Kat to the airport.

Kat plans to bring eight bags of luggage on the plane, not including the stuff that Thomas promised to ship to her new address. I have no idea how Kat will manage to shuffle so many bags through customs. And the rain might cause delays on the highway.

By the time Janusz arrives, the rain comes down hard. I see thunder and lightning and black clouds. A thick mist coats the skyline.

Janusz enters the apartment and scratches his head. Kat answers his silent question.

"Not all this stuff goes. Just the ones in the corner, close to the front door."

"I see," Janusz shrugs.

Janusz scrambles to haul the luggage down to his car. He only has lunch hour to help Kat before he must return to work.

Janusz speeds the car along the Gardiner Expressway. It's 2 p.m. and the flight leaves a little past three. Kat sits in the back seat, surrounded by suitcases and paraphernalia. She holds my hand. I small-talk with Janusz in the front seat. We strain to keep the conversation light.

Traffic slows to a halt.

"We might not be able to make it," I say.

Janusz is unfazed, "Don't worry about a thing. I'm sure we'll be able to make it fine. Sometimes, it's better not to have these thoughts weighing you down."

Janusz winds his way between cars and jerks the accelerator. I wonder how he manages to be both efficient and philosophical at the same time. Janusz has been studying Zen and meditating for over thirty years.

By the time we get to the airport, there are fewer than twenty minutes until departure. Kat and I gather all the luggage together and roll to the curb. Janusz waves goodbye and drives back to work.

Kat and I line up for customs. The customs officers give us long faces as we heave Kat's enormous luggage onto the metal scales.

The clerk at the counter pulls out a walkie-talkie, as if she's about to signal security. "First of all, this piece is way too heavy for carry-on, and you are beyond capacity. Second, you should have come much earlier. You are delaying the flight, ma'am."

Kat can only take five of the eight pieces of luggage with her.

Kat's eyes dart between the bags, trying to decide which to discard. "What should I do?" she asks me.

"Leave them with me," I say. "I can return them when I visit you in China. How's that?"

Kat appraises my skinny body and the heavy bags around her, "How the hell are you supposed to manage that? Look at you. And you don't even have a car!"

A burly guy in a white suit interjects, "Lady, you need to make a decision, or this plane leaves without you."

The clerk lady stands behind him, arms folded.

"Alright, already," Kat snaps. "Can't you see I'm having a hard time? What the fuck." Kat wrings her hands and rolls her eyes at me.

I look down at the luggage and decide which ones are most manageable. I say, "I'll take two of the lighter ones and the heavy one with all your makeup in it. Does that work?"

"How am I supposed to go without makeup?"

"You look fine without it."

Kat cracks a smile, "Okay, fuck. Deal. But you have to promise me that the gold-capped Lancômes get shipped to my new address, pronto. That shit is super expensive."

"Deal," I say.

Before I can continue, the burly guy is back. He tugs Kat's arm. It's time to go.

Kat looks at me with pity. We don't have a chance to say goodbye.

"I will text you?" I say.

"Yeah, okay." Kat looks at me one more time before she rolls her pink suitcase down the ramp. I heft the travel bags across both shoulders.

By the time I reach the escalator, I am ready to kick Kat's suitcases down the steps. The makeup is too heavy for me. My back aches. Stiffness fills my joints.

On the cab ride back, I see a missed call from Kat.

Janusz calls me. "Kat called, she's really upset. She saw you with the luggage. She just wanted to know that you were okay."

I call Kat but don't get through the first time. I call again. Kat answers. She speaks between sobs, "I was worried about you. I was just wondering if you're okay. You looked like you were having a hard time back there."

"It's okay. I managed to find a cab, and it looks like things are okay. Don't worry about me, dear. I will leave your stuff in my apartment until I figure out how to ship it."

"Okay," Kat sniffles. "I'm about to get on the plane now. It's gonna cut out on me soon. Talk to you later, okay?"

"Okay."

The phone cuts out.

I flip open my phone again, not knowing how to complete the moment. My fingers fumble over the keypad.

"I love you, Kat," I text.

A few moments pass before I hear the familiar vibration.

"I love you, too."

Later in the week, I contact Kat on Skype.

"Things are good," Kat says, "but there's only one thing."

"Yeah?"

"It's the landlord in Toronto. He left me a message the other day. Man, is he ever livid. He was complaining to me that I left so much stuff behind and he has to clean it up and stuff."

"I figured that," I said. "But I did what I could to get the stuff you needed. He's probably going to need a crew of cleaners to take care of the rest. Plus, he has to rent to a new tenant."

"I know. But I don't get why the landlord is so whiny. I can't help it. Can't he understand that I can't take everything with me?"

After Kat hangs up, I look around at the things I salvaged— term papers, Hunter boots, high-heeled shoes. I make a list of what goes and what stays.

The Road to Harlow

Michael Graham

S hould we try and call Tyler again?" Kendra leans back in the
passenger seat of the car, her feet resting on the dashboard.

Randy drives. I look out the window. Outside, the green fields
bordered by the thick hedgerows and low stone fences of rural
England whiz by.

"Will he actually pick up?" I say. I flip through Randy's 'Rise
Against' playlist on his battered iPhone 5S.

"Probably not, but you might as well try," says Randy from the
driver's seat. "Turn it down a bit, Smelly."

"Give it here, Pads." Kendra reaches her arm back, fingers
groping for the iPhone.

Kendra and Randy have called me Pads since I arrived in
England three days ago. Pads stands for Padfoot, the nickname
for Sirius Black in the Harry Potter novels, also my online mon-
iker. Randy, Tyler, and I met in an online, role-playing chat-room
around the time I started high school, ten years ago. We spent
most of our high school years writing together from the perspec-
tives of our favourite characters, and we bonded over our stories.
Randy still calls me by my character's name rather than my own.

Kendra, his girlfriend, caught on quickly.

I hand over the phone. Kendra taps the volume bar and slides it down. I pull out my tiny HTC One V phone and scroll through my contact list. I find "Tyler Kingston" and hit the green call button. It rings.

"Anything?" asks Randy.

I shake my head.

"Doesn't surprise me," says Kendra. "He's been really weird about not picking up his mobile lately. I haven't actually talked to him since that party you Skyped in for, I don't think."

"Oh yeah?" I say. "That's weird. We used to talk all the time."

"Yeah, he's been like that for the last little bit," says Randy. We stop for a roundabout. A white sign reads "Harlow" and points to the left. Randy flicks his indicator on.

"Wonder why that is," I say.

The light turns green. We shoot forward into the roundabout, loop around to the left, and turn onto a long, single-lane road.

"Dunno. He said he was excited to see you, though. We called him to check, two days before you flew in."

"Hopefully he'll be home, then," I say.

"If he isn't, I'll show him a thing or two," says Kendra. She glances over her shoulder at me and grins. I smile back.

"Oooh," says Randy. "Wouldn't want to get on your bad side, Smelly."

Kendra sticks her tongue out, "Shut up, Stinky."

Green fields, hedgerows three-feet high, and a mélange of cows, horses, sheep, and goats pass in a blur. Harlow, the town where Tyler Kingston lives, emerges on the horizon, and I stare out the window at the long lines of red and yellow brick Victorian houses. I wonder how Tyler will act in real life and if he will be home when we get there.

Tyler spoke the least in our online group chats. He only offered his input when asked, or when he had an extraordinary idea. Randy, a year younger than me, goofed around by sending cheeky ":P" faces and playing troublesome characters who got up to crazy antics. I, as the oldest of the group, popped in with new ideas whenever they came to me and I needed help fleshing them out.

I look forward at Randy. I take in his long, messy, brown hair, his green Legend of Zelda T-shirt, and his baggy grey pants that resemble the kind I used to wear in karate class, complete with a waist tie. He wears several dark wristbands, a Celtic ring on his middle finger, and two silver ones on his ring finger. He smirks over his shoulder at me.

Randy's Fiat hums as we drive into Harlow. The Victorian buildings that once stood in the distance now rise up on both sides of us. They pass by and give way to more modest and modern storefronts as we cruise down Harlow's long and empty High Street. We pass a small Tesco Express jammed between a Poundland and a Games Workshop, a short string of farmer's market stalls, and a mother chasing her three children down the street.

Randy turns a sharp left, and we lean in as he whizzes around the corner. He pulls out into the centre of the street to dodge cars parked on either side. Inches separate the sides of Randy's Fiat from the doors of the other cars. We veer back into the left lane as a Prius passes in the opposite direction. I turn to watch it slide through the narrow channel.

"Man," I say. "It's a good thing that Prius wasn't there when we were going through."

"Yeah," says Randy. He chuckles, "You get used to that pretty quick when you live here, I think. The streets were built back in Victorian days. Built for horses and shit. Nowadays there's not enough room to drive, let alone park."

"I can see that."

"Parking is a bitch anywhere in England," says Kendra. "Just wait 'til we go to Randy's. It's bloody ridiculous. Half the time, we have to park a few blocks away and walk, which is fucking horrid for my knees, of course."

I spy the metal bracelet on Kendra's arm. A snake winds its way around a shaft bearing wings on either side of it. "MEDIC ALERT" crosses the bottom of the logo. Kendra reclines in her seat, staring down her nose and out the window.

Kendra has medical conditions I can't remember the names of. I know that the simple act of walking is enough to cause permanent damage to her muscles, bones, and nerves. She once told me, laughing, that she broke a toe putting on a pair of socks. I remember the way Kendra gripped the banister on her way down the stairs earlier today. She insisted Randy and I go first. She told us to catch her if she blacked out, then she laughed and called herself troublesome.

Randy takes a hand off the wheel and reaches for Kendra's hand. He squeezes it. She smiles and rests her left hand on her stomach. She doesn't take her eyes off the road.

Randy makes a right turn. The buildings beside us spread apart. We descend towards long rows of semi-detached houses, each bordered by even strips of dull, flat grass. The houses, much like the apartments back on the High Street, exhibit nearly identical features—simple, white facades, tall, slanted roofs, and short awnings above plain, wooden doors. Some have garages, most do not.

Randy turns into a driveway.

"We're here,' he says. "Damn, I haven't been here in ages."

I gaze out the window at Tyler's house. A simple, golden wind chime dangles from the awning above the door. Several potted plants line the short, stone walkway through the garden and up to the door. The shutters hug the front of the house, mostly obscuring a dark room behind the foggy front window.

I rub my fingers together. I swallow. I cross my index finger over my middle finger.

We step out of the car. Randy stands beside it and looks up at the house. I move to stand beside him. He glances sidelong at me, a smile on his lips. "Never thought this'd happen, eh?" he says.

I shake my head. "We always talked about it, joked about meeting each other on one side of the pond or the other," I say.

"Yeah."

"Anyway, let's just hope he's here."

Randy nods. He stuffs his hands into his pockets and approaches the front door. Kendra hobbles after him. I linger for a moment, then follow. Randy knocks on the door. A bird chirps. The far-off rumble of cars thundering down the M-11 motorway fills the otherwise silent town.

Randy knocks again. We raise eyebrows at each other.

Kendra leans against the wall. She exhales.

Randy turns to Kendra, "Y'alright, Smelly?"

Kendra groans, "Yeah."

Randy turns to the door. I put my hands in my pockets. I cross my fingers harder. Randy knocks. The door opens. A pale, blue-eyed man with curly, blond hair emerges from the darkness within. He wears a thick, black sweater and ragged, dark-wash jeans. He stares at me. He peers over at Randy, then at Kendra.

"Oh," the man says. "Hey."

"Hey," says Randy. He grins, "Figured we'd drop by. Pads wanted to say hello."

Kendra smiles. I grin at Tyler.

Tyler smiles back, "Oh, right then. Uh, right. Come in!"

Randy and I look back at each other. Randy reaches out for Kendra's hand as they enter. I follow Tyler, Randy, and Kendra inside. We squish into his tiny mudroom, kick off our shoes, and shuffle through the pinched doorway into the living room. Tyler leads us through, gestures toward two squat, velvet couches, and smiles.

"Have a seat," says Tyler. "Do you guys want anything? Tea, or . . . ?"

"A cuppa, if you don't mind." Kendra lifts her index finger into the air with a grin. She drags herself to one of the couches and plunks down.

"Yeah, go on," says Randy. He joins Kendra on the couch and slides an arm across the back of her shoulders.

"Tea works," I say.

Tyler nods and disappears into the kitchen. I take a seat on the other couch, facing the small, glass coffee table and the tiny, wall-mounted, Panasonic plasma TV. I rest an arm on the armrest. I cross my feet. Randy shifts in his spot on the other couch.

Water boils and the electric kettle beeps in the kitchen. I hear a shuffling of feet and the clink of mugs. Tyler reenters the living room, each hand gripping two mugs. He distributes the mugs and then sits himself in the lone armchair that faces Randy and Kendra's couch.

I turn to Tyler. He holds his steaming cup of tea over his lap and smiles at me.

"Sorry," he says. He shakes his head.

"For what?" I raise an eyebrow.

"Earlier. I just . . . wasn't expecting it."

"Wasn't expecting what?" I ask.

"I guess I wasn't expecting to ever meet you."

Tea with Ajinder

Laura Raymond

I sip the hot cup of tea Ajinder poured me and smile as I scan her living room. Photographs of her five children cover the walls, bookshelves, and two side tables. Scattered between family photos are Toronto Maple Leafs posters, stickers, and signed postcards. Ajinder is the mother of one of my closest friends, Amar, who I met at the University of Ottawa during our first undergraduate year over fifteen years ago. Every time I visit her home, Ajinder welcomes me with a warm hug, ensures I am well fed, and sends me home with an old yogurt container filled with saag paneer or chicken curry.

Ajinder arrives with a second cup of hot tea for herself and sits down beside me. I ask her to tell me about her life.

———

I grew up in a small village called Chaminda in northwest India with my three older siblings—my sister Ashma and my two brothers, Bhavjeet and Dharampal. My mother was an angel, taking care of us kids while my father was away a lot of the time working hard to provide for our family. My father spent forty years of his life working as a wireless operator on a cargo ship out of Hong Kong, often travelling to places like Japan and the United States. He wanted to provide my siblings and me with the money we needed to get a good education. We were all able to go away to school, which not many people in our village were able to do at that time. My sister, Ashma, was the only girl from our whole village who got both her BA and her BEd. She immigrated to Canada when I was seventeen, and then she helped me to immigrate here in 1968, when I was just twenty-two years old.

After living with my sister for two years in Kamloops, British Columbia, I went back to India to find a husband. This was forty years ago. It's not like now. I had to marry an Indian man back then. My parents put an advertisement in the local newspaper that said I was a Canadian immigrant looking for a husband who was a mechanical or electrical engineer. My sister told me I should marry an engineer because he would be able to afford me a good future. My parents received one hundred and fifty responses to their advertisement from all over the country. Each response came with a letter and a picture of the potential husband.

My parents didn't bother going to see any of the boys in the letters, as many of them lived a great distance away, and my father didn't want to spend the money to get to them. One day, I happened to come across one of the letters lying around our home, and when I opened it I saw that the boy came from a nearby village only a few miles away. I told my father he wouldn't have to travel far to see him, and he agreed to go and introduce himself.

My father and one of my brothers went to meet the boy and his family. They decided they liked him enough. His family came to meet me. They decided they liked me enough, too. Our families were ready to arrange our engagement, but I asked my brother if

I could talk to this guy I was going to marry first. We only got to talk for two minutes. What can you learn about a person in two minutes? I felt a lot of pressure from our families, and so I agreed to marry him.

After we married in India, my new husband and I returned to Canada. We moved into my sister's house in Kamloops, and I got pregnant almost right away with my first daughter, Maya.

The mental and emotional abuse started soon after we arrived, when I told my husband about a friend I had in college who was a boy. It was just a friendship, nothing more. But my husband told me he didn't believe it was just a friendship. He told me I was a bad person, and he accused me of being physically involved with this boy. He told me that, no matter what I said, there was no way I could prove that nothing happened. He constantly put me down. My husband had been physically involved with plenty of women before me, but it was okay for men to do that. Women were not allowed to have any relationship with another man, even a friendship.

I was pregnant, living with an abusive husband I barely knew, and starting to feel very depressed. One night I took a handful of sleeping pills. I wanted to kill myself. My sister and my husband found out and took me to a hospital where the doctor made me throw up several times. I ended up being okay, and my baby was okay, too, thank God. After that, my husband suggested we move to Calgary, Alberta, for a fresh start. It was in Alberta that he started abusing me physically, too.

I told my brothers about the beatings, and they came and took me away. They brought me back to my sister's house in Kamloops, where I had a healthy baby girl. My sister's husband wasn't happy to have me back with a newborn, colicky baby who stayed up crying most of the night. He was the man of the house, and because he didn't like having baby Maya and me there, we had to leave. I went to my cousin's house first, then to my brother's house in Vancouver. My husband found out I was staying at my brother's house and showed up drunk, crying and pleading to have me back. I felt like a burden on my family, moving from house to house with my now two-month-old baby, so I gave in and returned to him. We moved to Nepean, Ontario, to be closer to his family.

I decided that this was my life. I wasn't going to bother anyone with the pain I suffered. If I lived, if I died, this was my life and I refused to be a burden on anyone, especially my own family.

———

I had four daughters before I had my son. Each time I had a girl, my husband wept with tears of disappointment. When I was five months pregnant with my fourth child, an ultrasound showed us we would have another girl. My husband wanted to send me to India to have an abortion, because no one would do an abortion in Canada at five months. But, before I got on the plane, he decided not to send me after all. I don't know what happened, but maybe God changed his mind.

We had four beautiful girls altogether: Maya (Mahanjot), Amar (Amarjit), Preeti (Gurpreet), and Jess (Jasdeep). Six months after Jess was born, I got pregnant again. This time, my husband sent me to Detroit where they could check if we were having a boy or a girl much earlier in the pregnancy, at just twelve weeks along. Thank God we found out we were having a boy, because if we were having another girl, I don't know what would have happened.

The night our son, Navi (Pranav), was born, I had to call a relative who lived close by to drive me to the hospital. My husband threw a big party with his friends and co-workers, but never showed me any kind of happiness or joy. I remained alone at the hospital.

I thought once I had a boy my husband would change—the abuse would end. But it only got worse. When my husband started abusing my eldest daughter, I knew I had to make it stop.

———

One night, Maya snuck out with her friends to a club in Gatineau, Quebec. She was about sixteen years old at the time. My husband's nephew, Balraj, was at the same club and called my husband to tell him Maya was there. My husband ordered Balraj to bring her home right away.

I was sleeping in the master bedroom with my nine-year-old daughter, Preeti, when my husband woke me up and slapped me across my face three times. He told me I was turning my daughters into prostitutes because I was spoiling them and couldn't control them. He had been drinking. He was angry and his eyes burned with hostility.

Balraj dragged Maya home. She tried to run away a few times, hoping she could get to the police. Maya knew what waited for her at home. But Balraj was a big guy—over six feet tall—and Maya couldn't escape him. When they got to the house, my husband opened the door and lured her inside with soft, false words, "Come inside. I'm not going to hurt you."

I told Maya to sleep in the master bedroom with me that night because we had a lock on the door, and I thought it would keep my husband away from her at least for the night. I told Balraj he had to sleep in the bedroom with us so he could protect Maya, and he agreed. That night, Maya and I slept on the bed, while Balraj slept on the floor. I'm not sure where my husband stayed.

In the morning, my husband calmly asked me to open the door. He walked over to where Maya lay, dragged her by her hair, and threw her down on the floor. He sat on top of her back with her face pressed into the floor, and he beat her. She couldn't breathe, so she turned her face to the side for air. He punched her on the side of her face, again and again. I made Balraj get him off of her. It was all such a blur, I can't remember exactly what happened next. I think my husband stayed in the room and we went downstairs, but I can't be sure. Sometimes you don't want to remember.

———

Maya started acting out, skipping a lot of classes. My husband made an appointment to meet with her principal about it. Maya was so scared that I decided to meet with the principal before her father got there. During the meeting, I opened up about how my husband had been beating us. The principal called the police, and two investigators came right away to take statements from both me and Maya. When my husband arrived for his appointment later that afternoon, he was arrested in front of the school on five separate charges.

That night, we didn't want to go back to our house. We were afraid my husband would get released from jail and come hurt us, or worse, try to kill us. The police arranged for us to stay at a motel in downtown Ottawa, far from our Nepean home. We returned to the house briefly, packed garbage bags with clothes and whatever else we needed, climbed into our van, and drove downtown.

The motel was very shady, and I wasn't comfortable staying there with my five children. It didn't feel safe, and we were already so frightened. Maya was becoming such a strong young woman, and she took it upon herself to find a shelter we could move to the next day. I don't know what I would have done without Maya during that time—she gave me so much strength.

We stayed in the shelter, in Kingston, for a few weeks, then moved to a shelter in Toronto that was run out of a convent. We wanted to get as far away from my husband as possible. We stayed at the cold, barren convent for a week before moving into a community housing complex that Maya found with the help of the nuns. We lived off the local food bank.

A few months after moving into the community housing complex, my second eldest daughter, Amar, needed to make an orthodontist appointment back in Nepean. I loaded three of my daughters—Amar, Preeti, and Jess—into our blue, Ford Aerostar van and began the drive up Highway Seven. Maya stayed home and took care of Navi. Not far into our drive, we hit a patch of black ice that caused our car to skid and then roll several times into a ditch. Amar was ejected from the vehicle and hit a snowbank. Firefighters had to pry Preeti, Jess, and me out of the van. I was conscious when they pulled me out of the wreckage, and I saw Amar lying across the road. I thought I had killed her. She woke up six hours later in the hospital during an MRI scan, thank God.

My husband was called during Amar's six-hour coma, and it re-opened our dialogue.

———

The kids and I moved back to our home in Nepean and lived in the basement while we rented out the main two floors. My husband rented a basement apartment of his own close by, and even though he was court-ordered to stay away from us, we let him see us sometimes. He took us out for nice dinners, bought us all lots of presents, and even bought me an $8000 fur coat. He wanted to win back our trust, and I'm sure he wanted us to drop the charges still pending against him. His wish was granted, because when the prosecutors and private investigators came looking for us to testify against him, we hid from them. We were afraid of the consequences, and we hoped that maybe he had changed. Eventually, all the charges against my husband were dropped.

————

In April of 1997, I thought we could try living together again. We stopped renting out our house's main floors, and my husband moved back in. It was two years since we left him, and I thought maybe he had changed.

He hadn't changed a bit.

He was still drinking hard liquor, heavily, every day. He still expected my daughters and me to bring him trays of food while he lay in bed, drank, and watched television. On Sundays, we had to bring him breakfast, lunch, and dinner in bed.

On Christmas Day, he got angry for some reason. I can't remember why. He was very drunk. He stood at the top of the stairs and roared, "Somebody's gonna get killed!"

I called Maya, who was away at Wilfrid Laurier University, and asked her what I should do. Maya told me to take all the kids and sleep in Amar's bedroom with the door locked.

The next day, he apologized. We tried to forget it, but you never really forget.

————

Eventually, I found the strength to leave my husband for good. I stood at the bottom of the stairs and told my children that I felt like a shell of a person, and that I was going to a shelter. I asked who wanted to come with me. All four children, still living at home, came with me.

We lived in shelters and we lived in cramped basements, but we persevered and moved forward. My children kept me going. They are my strength.

Today, I'm divorced, I'm a grandmother, I have a home of my own, and I have five incredibly intelligent, strong, and determined children. My children don't have limitations—I give them freedom to be who they are, to find happiness in whatever they want, and to choose their own partners no matter what race or culture. I encourage an open dialogue between us. I trust them, I love them, and I want them to talk with me like they could to a friend. I want them to feel that they can tell me anything. I always tell them the truth, and if I see that a man isn't treating one of my daughters well, I let them know. I want them to realize their own worth.

I'm not afraid to live a happy life anymore. I'm a huge Maple Leafs fan. I bought a sixty-inch TV so that I can watch my Leafs on the big screen. I love my Leafs. I've also been talking to men on shaadi.com, an Indian dating website. I'm going to visit my daughter Jess, who lives in Paris, next month. And a man I've been chatting with online is going to meet me there from England. It's kind of exciting.

I'm a survivor. I survived a marriage that knocked me down over and over again. I survived major surgery last year when I had to have three benign tumours removed from my neck. I will keep surviving and living every day I am on this earth.

I'm not ashamed of anything that's happened to me. I'm not ashamed of my difficult past. I shared my story with a young woman I know from work, and it helped her open up about her own abusive relationship. Since then, I've helped her and her three

children leave her husband and seek help. I've learned that sometimes, if you talk about your past, you can help someone else's
future. Our experiences make us who we are, and with the help of
my children, my experiences have given me the courage to stand.

Rate Me

Stefanie Turner

I Google my name. A media studies lesson plan I stumbled across last week suggested the practice. I decide I should try the exercise before introducing it to my eighth-grade students. I discover that my name has been added to ratemyteacher.com. It is the first and only hit that appears on Google under the search of my name.

Pop-up windows and advertisements for live–sex chats litter the web page after I click the link. My name stands in large, blue, block letters along with, "Cedar Hills Academy, Montreal, QC." Underneath are 3.5 gold stars and the phrase, "1 rating." My fingertips hover over the trackpad of my laptop, lower, and then graze downwards. My eyes scan the review. Several seconds pass before my brain interprets the meaning.

"May 10th, 2013: All she does is sit at her desk and yell at the same kids. Used to be hot and skinny but now she is so fat. Should start using the treadmill. I don't know how her zipper doesn't burst.

Humiliation flushes my face. I scrunch my eyes closed and press my palms into my eyelids until I see black and stars. I open my eyes and see nothing but white spots, and I don't want to see anything else, but gradually, the orange and blue letters of the page adjust back into focus. My hands rest on my stomach. I grab at the flesh. I think of Mark and his new girlfriend, and I wonder if this is why he dumped me. I open his girlfriend's Facebook page and look at their engagement picture. She is so tiny.

In the morning, I call Champlain Taxi as I scramble to pack my leather bag for the day. I don't have enough time to take the 55 bus to school. A pile of shift dresses, cardigans, pencils skirts, and self-loathing rests on my bed. I select black pants and a loose, long sweater. I skip breakfast.

I wear my shame throughout day. I look over my students' heads at the white crack in the far wall while I teach. They think I am looking at them. I taught them this trick during a public speaking unit in February.

At the end of the day, my students file out of our basement classroom. I stare at their backs and wonder which one of them hates me.

Once home, I work myself up for it, like a runner practicing starts before a race. My chest tightens, and I dim the lights so that everything is a little hidden. My closed laptop sits on my bed. I pace away from the computer, move towards the glass windows lining the south wall of my condo, and gaze at the lights of the apartments across the train tracks. My stomach muscles tighten and contract. I focus on slowing down my breath, hoping it will have a similar effect on my pulse.

I stride back to my bed, snatch the laptop, hurry over to the couch and drop into it, cross my legs, and pry open the computer lid. My fingers dance across the keys as muscle memory inputs the website's address. I hit Enter, clench my eyes shut, hold my breath, and wait for the screen to load.

I exhale. Nothing has changed since last night. I hover over the Report Comment icon. I check the box marked "commentary on physical appearance." Before sending the review, I must type the letters I see in the security box. It takes me three tries. My hands shake.

I plan to close the window, but my cursor travels to the top of the page and lands on the Rate This Teacher button. I click. I enter five stars for each category. Five for Clarity, five for Helpfulness, five for Easiness. I go back. Three for Easiness. I type in the comment box,

"Organizes good lessons and is always free for extra help if u need it. She is fun and makes class interesting. Great teacher!"

I submit the comment and refresh the page. After several seconds, my words and the five gold stars I awarded myself reflect back at me. Heat and shame flush my face. I report my own comment and close my laptop.

Anna's Hair

Loredana Polidoro

I met Anna five years ago in a cycling class at our local gym. We chatted often about food and our shared Italian culture.

I interview Anna at her home in Bloor West Village. We sit at her kitchen table. I nurse a coffee. Anna, a petite woman, wears black-framed glasses and sits across from me, sipping Pinot Grigio and smoking a cigarette.

"Can you tell me when you started to lose your hair?"

Anna takes in a deep breath and exhales as she begins her story.

"Two years ago, when I was on a beach vacation with my girl-friend. She spotted a little bald spot on the back of my head, near the bottom of my neck. I was scared to death. It reminded me of when I was thirteen years old and lost a portion of my hair. But I thought everything would be fine. I went to the doctor to have it checked out, and within four months I was completely bald."

"My dermatologist diagnosed me with Alopecia Areata, an autoimmune disease. People usually get alopecia when they are younger. It's not as common for adults to get it. With the type I have—Areata—it's more common to get bald spots. It's rare to go completely bald. I went completely bald and even lost all my body hair." Anna shrugs her shoulders and sinks deeper into her seat. She looks up and smiles. "Above the neck I want it back, below the neck I don't."

"Did the dermatologist tell you what caused it?" I ask.

"They don't know exactly. I was told it could be brought on by a sudden stress or perhaps something that occurred in my past—like post-traumatic stress. When it started to happen to me, besides the day-to-day stresses, everything was fine. I've always had a very happy life."

Anna continues, "My doctor referred me to an endocrinologist to investigate if it was internal. I was tested for everything. All the results came back clean. They still don't know exactly why it happened to me."

Anna takes a drag from her cigarette and blows the smoke out of the side of her mouth.

"But, I have some theories of my own." Anna leans in closer.

"When I lost my hair at thirteen, I got my period. Now I'm in my early fifties and going through menopause. Both incidents happened when my body was going through a change. I've self-diagnosed myself that it's hormonal." Anna leans back in her chair and flicks the ashes of her cigarette in the ashtray. She takes one last draw from the cigarette and butts it out.

I ask, "Is there a treatment for it?"

"I see my dermatologist every three weeks for injections into my scalp. The injections are supposed to stimulate the follicles. I also apply an ointment every night. And sometimes, I use Rogaine, a hair cream for men, even though I've been told not to."

"Can you describe the injections?"

"They are horrible." Anna squeezes her eyes shut and shakes her head. "The whole day takes a lot out of me, physically and emotionally. Before the dermatologist starts the injections, he gives me a tension ball to squeeze for the pain. The pain doesn't last that long, though. By the time I'm halfway home, I just have a little headache. The worst part is sitting in the room waiting to see the doctor. I have to take my wig off and wait for the doctor and his medical assistant. It's usually some beautiful young girl with flowing hair. The girls look startled when they see me without my hair."

"When did you get your wig?"

"Back when I still had eyebrows, eyelashes and a few wisps of hair. I searched online for wig places in Toronto. I found Continental Hair in Yorkville. They specialize in wigs for people who have cancer or alopecia."

"They were the first ones to tell me I would probably lose my eyebrows and eyelashes. That was devastating."

"Mike, the stylist who helped me, took the time to sit with me on my first visit, tell me about the wigs, and find one that was right for me. I tried on a lot of wigs in that visit. I felt overwhelmed and got emotional. They were beautiful wigs but they were gross. It felt gross. It wasn't my hair. It's difficult to find curly hair in a wig, so I had to get one with straight hair." Anna runs her fingers through the ends of her hair.

Anna picks up her wineglass and continues, "It's still hard, though. But I've been lucky. My family has been supportive, and my boyfriend has been amazing. My biggest fear when this started to happen was that he wouldn't want to be with me. My physical appearance changed so much. I used to have beautiful, curly hair. I was known for my hair. That was me. My personality was the hair. Everything was the hair. Now I am completely bald. No eyebrows, no eyelashes. I'm an alien. I look in the mirror and think, 'I wouldn't want to be with me.' But my boyfriend doesn't care. He supports me and still tells me I'm beautiful."

"How many people know about the alopecia?"

"Close family and friends know, but I don't share it with everyone. They don't need to know. I'm sure there are people who noticed when I started to get bald spots. And I had curly hair. Then, all of a sudden, I had straight hair."

Anna sips from her glass and says, "When I first wore my wig to the office, I got so many compliments. People wanted to touch my hair. It was so strange. I was nervous about them pulling too hard and moving the wig. I didn't want them to know it was not my real hair, so I lied and told them that I had my hair chemically straightened."

"Who has seen you without your wig?"

"Besides my boyfriend, only my sister and nephew, and a few very close friends. But they haven't seen me without my eyebrows and eyelashes. They haven't seen the real alien. Only my boyfriend sees the real alien."

"I don't like people seeing me without my face. I'll put a hat on if I don't want to wear my wig at home, but I always put my face on. It's part of my morning routine. I get up and look like an alien, then I put on eyeliner and draw in my eyebrows. The eyebrows take the longest. They have to be even, so sometimes I have to wash them off and start again. It takes a long time to create a face that simulates what I used to look like. I hide my face behind glasses. I used to wear contacts, but when I lost my hair I switched to glasses."

"Has there been an improvement in your condition?"

"My eyebrows and eyelashes are starting to grow back, but not a lot. I put mascara on the couple of eyelashes that I do have," Anna bats her eyes to show me her new growth.

"Some days, I notice little hairs on the top of my head. But, by the next morning they usually fall out." Anna shrugs, "I still hope it's going to come back. My dermatologist is hopeful. I can't wait to walk down the street with a brush cut. I just want my hair back."

The Eye

Dani Buchner

I slouch in a stiff, brown chair and stare at the white, tiled floor of the waiting room. Ophthalmology occupies the entire fifth floor of Toronto Western Hospital.

I watch as a middle-aged woman struts out of the surgery hall in her heels, leather pants, and eye patch. Her curly hair falls around her face. The receptionist follows her out and escorts her back into the room. She places a phone call as the woman waits.

I pull my hair into a tight ponytail and fasten a Lululemon headband around my head to catch the flyaway hairs.

I look up at my dad, "Do you think I can take this anxiety pill now?" I shake the translucent bottle that contains a single, tiny, white pill. I drop my head between my knees and close my eyes. I sway back and forth.

Dad places his hand on my back, "You can probably just take it. Are you going to faint?"

I groan.

"Okay," the receptionist approaches, "you're next. Take the pill."

I place the tiny, white tablet under my tongue.

She leads me away from Dad to another waiting room. Doctors chat at the end of the hall. I eavesdrop.

"We've already had six emergencies today!"

I once heard emergencies happen in groups of seven. I am the last surgery of the day.

"She's the school teacher. I remember her."

Are they really talking about me? How do they remember that?

I gaze at posters of glaucoma and cataracts. I wait for the pill to kick in. I rest my head between my legs and close my eyes once more.

A girl dressed in green scrubs appears. "Danielle?" she asks. I follow her down the hall.

Spindly lights, metallic instruments, and magnifying lenses fill the cramped room. A large, beige chair covered in plastic sits in the centre. A tall stool waits next to it. Shelves full of eye drops, medical gauze, and syringes line the far wall. "Jingle Bell Rock" swings out of the radio. The doctor standing in front of me is not the one who did my pre-op.

I set myself down in the large, beige chair. The plastic squeaks.

"Is the music okay?" the doctor asks.

"Yep."

"I am Dr. Zvorgotsky. Did I do the pre-op with you?"

"No . . . ."

"Alright, well, we work as a team here. You must have had Dr. Mahabai. I will be doing your surgery today. You are here for a pterygium removal and conjunctivial graft, correct? Dr. Mahabai should have given you all of the information about the procedure, yes? You are going to be awake for the whole procedure, but you won't feel any pain. We will freeze your eye and the surrounding area. You will see light and shadows. You will feel touch but no pain. You will be fully aware, and we will be giving you instructions about where to look."

I nod, "Okay." I wonder when that pill is going to start working.

Eyedrops plop into my eyes and stream down my face.

Dr. Zvorgotsky stands over me. "I am going to give you this needle now."

I grab the sides of the armchair, "Can you just prepare me, you know, um, mentally? Where exactly are you going to put that needle?"

Dr. Zvorgotsky smirks, "Do you really want to know?"

I hesitate. I decide, "Nope."

Dr. Zvorgotsky pushes a squirt of liquid through the eye of the needle. "This will be the last pain you feel," he says.

The needle approaches my eye. I cannot see it by the time I feel it.

The room melts into a series of blacks, greys, and browns. A bright light burns and then disappears in the shadow of Dr. Zvorgotsky's hand.

"All done. Okay, now I need you to look to the left."

A light burns near the rim of my vision. I feel scraping and pressure. I hear scratching and snipping. "Silent Night" plays in the background.

I focus on my breath. I wonder what will happen if I faint. Will he slice my eye open by accident?

"Are you practicing yoga?" Dr. Zvorgotsky asks.

I stifle a laugh, "I'm just trying not to pass out."

Instruments clatter, drips trickle, light burns, and shadows swirl around my eye.

I consider how many songs have passed. I try to convince myself it has been a few, but I know it has been only one. The surgery is supposed to take fifteen minutes. That should be about four songs.

"You keep slipping downwards in the chair," Dr. Zvorgotsky says with surprise.

"I'm just really tense. Sorry."

Am I really the only person who gets nervous about eye surgery?

The song changes to "I'm Dreaming of a White Christmas." Pressure focuses on the inside part of my eye. The doctor's scissors clip at the fleshy, pink part, next to my nose. The clips sting.

"Are you almost done? I am starting to be able to feel what you're doing." My legs twitch involuntarily. I realize, and hold them still.

"We're getting there. I will give you more drops."

Splashes hit my eyes and the song changes. "It's Christmas Time" begins to play.

"I need you to look down now."

Light escapes from my vision. I know what he is doing. I have done the research. He slices the top of my eye to get the graft. I squeeze the sides of the chair. I feel pressure at the top of my eye. My face tickles with artificial tears.

"I am just going to glue on the graft, and then we are done."

I feel his fingers pressing on my eye.

"We just have to wait three minutes for the glue to settle."

"Okay," I heave a sigh of relief.

After three minutes, the doctor removes the clamp keeping my eye open and places on an eye patch. "You are done here. All set! Follow-up appointment in a week. Here's a prescription for your eye drops. Take them four times a day. Follow the instructions they come with."

The doctor stands in the doorway, "Take your time, just get up when you are ready."

He leaves.

My dad has to hold me as we exit the hospital. The brightness of the hallway hurts my good eye. I put on my sunglasses to block some of the light. I pull my hood up over my head to block out my peripheral vision. I direct my gaze at the floor, but I trip over flat tiles and head straight over steps. I shuffle through the hallways and let Dad guide the way.

Beginning

Shoshana Green

My leg twitches. A blind plinks against a window. A clock ticks. My eyes blink in the greyness. My skin gains awareness of the sheets as my mind gains awareness of reality. Where is he?

My senses locate his warmth, his scent, his breath. Near and asleep. My eyes close, and I fade in and out of consciousness. Waves of shock, confusion, panic, and release beat against me. With each tide of sensations, the greyness of the room lightens. A sterile sun rises.

His warmth, his skin against mine, and his breath through open mouth bring me to sleep.

———

A nurse enters. She checks both our vitals, gives me some pills, and squirts a syringe of bright red liquid into my mouth. Divalproex, a mood stabilizer, causes neural tube defects in newborns. For the last nine months, I have taken extra doses of folic acid and Effexor and crossed my fingers that my baby's spine would form properly.

———

"You're lucky to be in this program," says Dr. Rosen. "The hospital is very strict about which patients qualify. Six hours of sleep a night during the first five days is crucial to your mental health."

A calendar appears in my head with one square X'ed out and four more illuminated after.

"Thanks," I say. I push the corners of my mouth up and look away from the doctor as tears rush to my eyes.

My private room mirrors the semi-private room we started in. Dingy tiles and yellowed paint glare from the rectangle of space where the second bed should be. I imagined plush chairs, a dresser, maybe a throw rug. People call this place The Baby Hilton.

My eyes flutter open. The nurse wheels him in. It must be six in the morning. He lies in his plastic tub, swaddled, staring wide-eyed at me. I look into his dilated pupils and remember seeing them for the first time twenty-eight hours ago.

———

"Dad! Get down here!" The doctor called from the foot of the bed. His voice floated up from between my raised knees.

"Oh!" Jamie let go of my hand and disappeared past my waist.

"We have a son!" Jamie announced, and my breath caught in my throat, and a pit formed in my stomach, and I pushed against the disappointment and fought down the tears because new mothers don't get disappointed.

A gurgling wail quivered through the darkness.

"Is he okay?! He sounds like he's underwater," I said.

Fear gripped me and I couldn't believe how long it took for someone to answer, and my baby sounded like he was fighting for air, and no one was doing anything.

"That's what newborns sound like!" said Andrea, my friend and doula. I heard a smile in her voice.

"He sounds like a lamb bleating underwater," I said.

"Here you go, Mom!" Hands thrust toward me, holding tiny limbs pointed in different directions, and the lamp cast all of us in shadows.

"What is that?" I asked. Warmth sprayed over my shoulder and arm.

"He's peeing!" Andrea laughed.

I took this bundle in my hands and lifted the sheet, and half of a tiny face peeked out with wide, dark eyes, and I couldn't believe his eyes were open and he was here with me, calm and silent, alert and unexpected.

———

I reach for him now. He reaches back with his eyes, nose, and mouth. I dig him out of his cocoon and nestle him against me, under my gown. He searches for food.

———

"Take some extra socks to the hospital," said my co-worker, Krista, a few months before I went on maternity leave. "You use them to prop up the baby so you can breastfeed in bed. My midwife taught me that trick. That way you can sleep while he nurses."

"Sit in a chair with your feet on the floor. There are some step stools available if you need them," said the nurse at the breast-feeding clinic yesterday.

I raised my hand a little.

"Yes?" the nurse looked at me.

"What about breastfeeding in bed?" I said.

"I think you'll find it much easier to get into an upright position in a chair," the nurse said.

"No," I said, "I mean lying down." The nurse shook her head.

"A lot of moms I know said it's comfortable and that you can sleep while they nurse," I said.

"No," her head continued to shake, "that's really advanced. You and your baby aren't ready for that."

————

A vinyl recliner sits beside a metal locker at the foot of the hospital bed. The surface of the chair compresses when I sit on it. I put him back in the bucket while I fiddle with the rail on the bed, put on socks, and line the chair with pillows and blankets.

I bring him towards me. I watch his jaw, like they showed us in the prenatal class video. Sweat shoots from my hairline and lands in my eye. It startles me and I brace myself. I am terrified of dropping him. I wiggle my butt deeper into the recliner and I tilt the pillow and the baby toward me. "Don't let go," I think.

————

My eyes spring open. Was I sleeping? Holy shit. I can't fall asleep. If I fall asleep, my arms will go limp, and I'll drop the baby. I can't fucking drop this baby. Fuck, fuck, fuck. What time is it? 7:25.

I call home.

"Hello?" Jamie says.

"Hi," I say, "I guess you're not up yet."

"Almost. I'm getting there. Everything okay?"

"Yeah. Everything's fine. When can you come?"

"Probably around 10:30. I have to do some stuff around here. Feed the cats—"

"Can you come sooner?" I ask.

"Why, is something wrong?"

"No, nothing's wrong. We're just alone. I want you here with us."

"I will be, just not for a few hours."

"Fine. Bye," I say and hang up.

Three hours later. He nurses and falls asleep. I pull him off my breast and he cries. I keep switching sides. Both nipples throb and I just want to sleep, and why won't he sleep like he did yesterday?

Dr. Rosen, my psychiatrist, checks in each morning. She brings an intern today. They sit beside my bed. The intern watches, smiles, and keeps her eyes on me. Dr. Rosen tilts her clipboard and poises her pen. "How's your mood?" Dr. Rosen asks.

"It's fine," I say. I exhale and look at the wall to the left of Dr. Rosen's face.

"Yeah?" The corners of Dr. Rosen's mouth lift, and the corners of her eyes crease. "Is he eating?"

"Yeah," I say, "he won't stop." My eyebrows draw together.

"Cluster feeding," Dr. Rosen says.

I stare down at my hands, "Yeah, I know. That's what it's supposed to be, but he really won't stop. I'm not sure he's getting enough."

"Why don't you give him formula?" Impatience creeps into Dr. Rosen's voice.

"I might. I don't know. We have an appointment with a breastfeeding consultant this afternoon." I work to maintain even breathing and still features.

"Just give him formula, Shoshana. I gave my baby formula in the hospital. She was starving!"

"I want to try to feed him myself," I say and feel my throat twitch.

"Okay," she says. "But your mood's okay?"

"Yes."

I take walks because the doctors and my mother tell me to. I pass posters in the hall that say newborns only need a few drops of colostrum, the nutrient-rich early breast milk, in the first couple of days.

———

Day Four. I am going home. I have made my decision. I rehearse my speech as I wait for Dr. Rosen's daily visit.

My medications have quadrupled. Not only am I back to my full dose of mood stabilizers, but now I have a fistful of herbal supplements to take with every meal. I'm not making enough milk. When I had breast reduction surgery ten years ago, I had no idea what supplementation meant. I had no idea that I had traded my hang-ups about cup size for hang-ups about formula feeding.

I have blisters around my nipples, and the breastfeeding consultant says she's never seen anything like them, and I find this hard to believe, and I explain that I fell asleep while he was nursing and he sort of slipped and he kept sucking but he wasn't getting anything, and at least we know he has good suction, and I wonder how you become a breastfeeding consultant and if you get training for bedside manner, and someone should write a handbook for boobs.

Dr. Rosen appears. She smiles and takes a seat, "How are you?"

"I'm good. I want to go home today," I say.

"Really? It's only day four. You have one more day. One more night of good sleep."

"I'm not sleeping well. I need Jamie. I'm by myself all morning. I'm exhausted, and I have no one to help me."

"If you're exhausted now, just wait until you get home," she says.

"I know. I'll have to wake up and feed and pump during the night, but I'll also have my mom and my husband to help me—to take turns holding him. I'm falling asleep holding him. I'm afraid I'm going to drop him."

"Wait, who said anything about pumping at night? That's mishigoss. Craziness."

"The consultants said I need to pump after every feeding," I say.

"Yeah, but they don't mean at night," she says.

"I'm pretty sure they do," I say.

"Shoshana, you're not a super-woman. You have to sleep."

"I know, but I have to feed my baby."

"So give him formula! Look, if you promise not to pump at night, I'll let you go home," Dr. Rosen says.

"Okay, fine."

———

Jamie gets him in the middle of the night. Jamie sterilizes the bottles. Jamie does everything that doesn't require boobs.

I sleep. He cries. I open one eye, peek at the clock, and listen. I fall back asleep until the cries get louder and more frequent. I drag my arms out from under the sheet and push myself up and reach into the crib. I try to stay upright and nurse on each breast for at least ten minutes before switching to formula. I try to pump for at least ten minutes on each side. I try to do this every time he wakes up, and sometimes he only sleeps for twenty minutes. During my pregnancy, everyone told me that I would wake when my baby made the slightest noise. Sometimes I open my eyes and I see him crying, and my eyelids close against my will, and my arms and legs feel like lead and I keep sleeping.